In The Mountains

The health and wellbeing benefits of spending time at altitude

Ned Morgan

In The Mountains

The health and wellbeing benefits of spending time at altitude

Ned Morgan

Dedicated to my parents, Jack and Linda Morgan.

An Hachette UK Company
www.hachette.co.uk

First published in Great Britain in 2019 by
Aster, a division of Octopus Publishing Group Ltd,
Carmelite House, 50 Victoria Embankment,
London EC4Y 0DZ
www.octopusbooks.co.uk

ISBN 978-1-78325-322-7

A CIP catalogue record for this book is available from the
British Library.

Printed and bound in China.

10 9 8 7 6 5 4 3 2 1

Consultant Publisher Kate Adams
Senior Editors Leanne Bryan & Louise McKeever
Designer Jack Storey
Contributing Editor Jo Smith
Illustrator Grace Helmer
Picture Research Manager Giulia Hetherington
Deputy Picture Manager Jennifer Veall
Production Manager Lisa Pinnell

Contents

INTRODUCTION   6

1. MOUNTAINS AND MANKIND   10

2. PHYSICAL HEALTH AT HIGH ALTITUDE   22

3. THE PSYCHOLOGICAL BENEFITS OF   42
   MOUNTAINS

4. A MOUNTAIN WAY OF LIFE   70

5. ENHANCING THE BENEFITS   110
   OF THE MOUNTAINS

6. BRINGING THE MOUNTAINS CLOSER   140
   TO HOME

7. THE FUTURE FOR MOUNTAIN RESEARCH   154
   AND CONSERVATION

REFERENCES   184
INDEX   188
FURTHER READING   191
PICTURE CREDITS   192
ACKNOWLEDGEMENTS   192

INTRODUCTION

～～～～～

"When the aromatic savour
of the pine goes searching
into the deepest recesses
of my lungs, I know it is life
that is entering."

— Nan Shepherd, *The Living Mountain*

In an increasingly urbanized world, high mountains still lie mostly beyond our reach. Of all earth's landscapes, none fixes our attention more than mountains. Why are we drawn to them? The following pages will attempt to answer this question and also present many reasons why mountains, in all their variety, are good for us in ways we're just beginning to understand. We will examine not just why being at higher altitude may improve our physical and emotional health, but also the evolution of mountains' meaning both in our shared myths and in our everyday lives.

The geological foundations of mountains reach far back in prehistory to an earth unrecognizable to us, constantly moulded and remoulded by a long series of tectonic stress events and volcanism: mass convulsions over billions of years with no human witnesses. Today's mountains serve as remnant monuments of this tumult. And they're also much more than that. One of the questions we hope to answer here is: why are mountains good for us and why should we care about conserving them? And how might they benefit us even if we live at sea level with no peaks in sight?

Mountains may seem forever fixed on our horizons even if the geologic change that created them is ongoing. But short of a volcanic eruption, a mountain will look the same to us throughout a human lifespan. Whether a mountain seems eternal to our eyes, or is exploding with smoke and lava, it commands our instant respect.

Inside a Cloud: My Background

A cloud in a balcony: that's how it started for me. One summer as a 17-year-old, I took a French language course at an international school in the village of Les Avants in the Bernese Alps above Montreux, Switzerland. The school was in the former Grand Hôtel, built in the 1870s to serve tourists arriving on the recently completed railway. Though still grand, the building had long ceased to be a hotel by the time I stayed there, the rooms mostly converted into multiple-bed dorms. But the balconies remained and from my fifth-floor room I looked out at an expanse of lime-green turf, dotted with lonely evergreens, rising up until it vanished from view, and the bare granite spire of Dent de Jaman in the middle distance. Several misty mornings I awoke to a cloud hovering in my balcony. Far away, faint choruses of cowbells echoed around the valley walls. I was inside a cloud, and my world was full of wonders.

Since then, mountains have been places for me to revive and inform my place in nature. Many years after Les Avants, now working as an editor and writer in the outdoor media industry, I was part of a cat-ski trip to British Columbia's Selkirk Mountains. On a bright day in January, on a snowbound alpine ridge, I found myself transfixed by the layer of clouds over the Lardeau Valley far below us. This opaque roof of pearl-tinted cloud swirled gently like a slow-motion whirlpool over the deep, narrow valley. Here above the clouds we took a moment to savour this perspective, and I felt a silent exhilaration. Then we descended into the untracked bowl, adrenaline swiftly overriding contemplation.

To someone like me who was born at sea-level, standing inside or looking down on clouds is one of the most immediate signals that mountains are a realm apart. In the following pages we will trace the myriad strands that begin here.

CHAPTER 1

MOUNTAINS AND MANKIND

~~~~~~~~~~

"Great things are done
when men and mountains
meet; This is not done by
jostling in the street."

— William Blake

Mountains cover at least 22 per cent of our planet's surface. Most geographers would agree that a mountain is a landform rising 300 metres (1,000 feet) or more above its immediate surroundings. If we broaden the definition to include highlands and hill country, the estimate of earth's total mountainous terrain could increase to more than 35 per cent. The immediate and iconic image of a mountain may be a snow-covered peak, but in fact they are complex and diverse landforms whose topographical isolation protects plant biodiversity crucial to agriculture and science.

There are major and minor mountains on every continent (and under the ocean) but the highest land systems are as follows:

- The Himalayas in central Asia, comprising three parallel ranges passing through India, Pakistan, Afghanistan, China, Bhutan and Nepal.

- The Alps in central Europe, which covers areas of France, Italy, Switzerland, Germany, Austria, Slovenia, Croatia, Bosnia and Herzegovina, Montenegro, Serbia and Albania.

- The North American Cordilleran System in western North America, including the Rockies.

- The Andes in western South America, including the Cordillera Oriental and Cordillera Occidental ranges.

THE SERVICES MOUNTAINS OFFER US

Both major and minor mountain systems provide ecosystem services which include, perhaps most importantly, delivering water to the lowlands. Up to 40 per cent of earth's population depends, directly or indirectly, on the irrigation and drinking water, as well as the hydroelectricity, that mountains provide. Mountains hold and cyclically release water from glaciers and snowpack. Due to higher precipitation rates in mountain areas, many major rivers originate here. To take just one example among many, ten of the largest rivers flowing out of the Hindu Kush Himalayas deliver water to more than 1.35 billion people at lower elevation.

High-altitude ecosystems and forests improve and balance air quality and climate, helping to protect human populations from droughts and floods. Roughly 1.2 billion people live in mountainous regions. And for many more people, mountains hold religious and cultural meaning; they also serve as hubs for tourism and recreation.

Mountains in Myth

Looking back at some of humanity's foundational stories, mountains loom high. In humanity's early myths, the mountain is a symbolic link between earth and the divine – a rough elevator to sacred realms. Many mythologies reference some sort of holy mountain, in a fabled time when humans could communicate with the god or gods atop it. One example, in the Hindu epic Mahābhārata, is the mythical Mount Meru: a gigantic mountain at the centre of the world and 'the seed cup of the world lotus' where multiple gods in Hindu cosmology reside. Mountain symbolism is pervasive across cultures and millennia. Many Native American peoples, particularly in the Pacific Northwest, saw mountains as giant ancestors, or as life-giving gods like Takhoma ('mother of waters'), as the Puyallup called what is now known as Mount Rainier in Washington State. In Dante's 14th-century narrative poem The Divine Comedy, paradise is located on top of Mount Purgatory.

As well as the gods themselves, other supernatural beings also reside on certain mountains, for example the Muses on Olympus. They were nine omniscient female deities of Greek myth who sang to the gods residing on Olympus and represented the faculty of memory. They guided the aimless mortals below who played lyre and composed poetry, offering them protection and inspiration – and teaching them to forget suffering and death for a time. Perhaps vestiges of these divine and redemptive associations live on in our conception of and association with mountains today.

Mountains symbolize a transition realm where humans may glimpse a place separate from earth and the afflictions of mortals. Mountains are still of the earth but, at their summit, the pilgrim, the climber or the dreamer may find an enlightenment that is unavailable below. Perhaps if we were to worship mountains (and climb them symbolically, as it were) we might be able to attain spiritual advancement and transcend our imprisoning human sphere in the process. Or perhaps it is possible that humans can communicate directly with the divine or receive a revelation on a mountaintop, as did Moses on Sinai, and the Prophet Muhammad on Jabal al-Nour.

To most ancient civilizations, high mountains were *terra incognita*, where humans could never hope to venture in a physical sense. Unsung mountain climbers in the distant past may have scaled a few peaks – after all, we know little of the Hindu pilgrims who bestowed the Sanskrit name Himalaya (*hima* for 'snow' and *ālaya* for 'abode') on the ranges they visited many centuries ago. But by and large in the West, mountains were abodes of gods and occasionally heroes – in Greek myth, for example, Jason was raised by a centaur on Mount Pelion in Thessaly.

~~~~~~~~~~~~

High-Altitude Pilgrimages

Often involving physical hardship, many of the noted pilgrimages of the world centre on shrines in isolated mountain regions.

Sansa Monasteries, Republic of Korea

Scattered throughout the Republic of Korea – a country roughly 65 per cent mountainous – are seven well-preserved mountain monasteries collectively known as the Sansa. In 2018 the United Nations Educational, Scientific and Cultural Organization (UNESCO) designated these Buddhist temples, which date back as far as the 7th century, a World Heritage Site. Located in lush forest settings on mountain slopes, most can be readily accessed on foot. Trekking in Korea is a well-established and nationally encouraged pastime. One of the largest structures, Beopjusa Temple, lies among the misty crags of Songnisan National Park.

Mount Canigou, France

In the Pyrénées-Orientales department of France – sometimes called Northern Catalonia – rises Mount Canigou, a 2,785-metre (9,100-foot) peak in the Pyrénées range. Every June before the Feast of St John, hundreds of Catalans ascend their sacred mountain, which is visible from the Mediterranean Sea and in ancient times served as a navigational aid. Though two early Medieval Catholic monasteries lie at Canigou's base, the annual pilgrimage known as the *Trobada* is not so much a religious ceremony as it is a nationalist celebration for the stateless Catalans. Arriving by mule, horse, bike, jeep or on foot, adorned in the red and gold colours of Catalonia, the pilgrims often carry bundles of sticks to feed the ritualistic summit fire, the *Flama del Canigó*.

Sulaiman-Too Mountain, Kyrgyzstan

An ancient place of pilgrimage, the multi-peaked Sulaiman-Too overlooks the city of Osh on the Silk Road, the former trade route between China and the Mediterranean. Honeycombed with caves and shrines, it is of major archaeological interest, with pre-Muslim petroglyph sites and two 16th-century mosques. The shrines – many of which are still in use and connected by footpaths – are thought to aid fertility, cure aches and pains, and bestow longevity. Sulaiman-Too is probably central Asia's most sacred mountain.

The Lake District, England

Cumbria, in the northwest of England, is home to not just the country's largest lake (Windermere) but also its highest mountain, Scafell Pike, at 978 metres (3,210 feet). The Lake District was the home of and primary inspiration to Romantic poet William Wordsworth (1770–1850), whose lyric poem *Daffodils* encapsulates what the place meant to him. Many other poets, writers and artists have also memorialized the wild beauty of the region – including Sir Walter Scott, Samuel Taylor Coleridge, John Ruskin and Beatrix Potter – and its sprawling massifs and deep-cut valleys are secular pilgrimage destinations. The shrines here are not religious; in recent years, hikers have established routes (including a 275km/171 mile loop) to numerous 'natural cathedrals' or spires of ancient volcanic rock.

Mountains in Fact

One mountain with the distinction of being both factual and celestial is the dome-peaked Mount Kailash (pictured) at 6,714 metres (22,000 feet), its summit technically in Tibet but its massif encompassing India, China and Nepal. Tibetan Buddhists revere the mountain as the home of Demchog, the 'One of Supreme Bliss', a multifaceted deity symbolizing enlightenment. Hindus, Jains and Chinese Buddhists also make pilgrimages to its base. By unspoken agreement, mountaineers have always steered clear of Kailash – no one, at least in recorded history, has dared to summit it. Though Mount Everest may tower above it in height and infamy, as a sacred site Kailash puts Everest in the shade.

With the first successful summit of Europe's highest peak Mont Blanc in 1786, the role of mountains in the West began to shift (though remnants of the divine-elevator will always remain). With peak after peak climbed, and flag after flag planted, mountains became jagged proving grounds for national pride. New Zealander Edmund Hillary and Nepalese Sherpa Tenzing Norgay summited Everest in 1953 and, the following year, an Italian team topped the world's second-highest mountain, K2, on the China-Pakistan border – a more difficult ascent.

By 1964, climbers had stood atop all 14 of the world's mountains over 8,000 metres (26,200 feet) in elevation, known as the 8,000ers (and all in the Himalaya). Today every last millimetre of earth's highest and remotest terrain is mapped and photographed. The world's highest peaks may have lost their mystique, but the need to climb them shows no sign of waning, even though the risks remain unabated. The deadliest-ever Mount Everest climbing season was 2015, with 24 deaths. Even with ideal weather and no earthquakes or major icefalls during the 2018 climbing season, Everest still claimed the lives of five.

Mountains and Self-Examination

Italian-born mountaineer Reinhold Messner – the first to summit all 14 of the 8,000ers, and without supplemental oxygen – is a proponent of minimalist alpine freestyle climbing. After summiting Everest without oxygen in 1978, and garnering comparisons to Hillary and Tenzing's 1953 first ascent, he explained: 'Their ambition was to stand on the summit. Mine was an adventure towards spiritual and ethical self-examination. We both succeeded. Hillary with his summit, and me with a new measure of myself.'[1]

After most available peaks have been conquered, spiritual and ethical self-examination may be the new object of mountaineering.

Overlooking a vast mountain range doesn't necessarily spur everyone to don crampons and climb. One doesn't need to scale a mountain to benefit in some way from the venture. The Death Zone can bring all manner of life experience into stark relief. How do we act when faced with tragedy or impossible choices? What is courageous and what is reckless? Accounts of humans enduring, and sometimes not enduring, in these environments may help to answer these and other big questions.

SAVOURING UNCERTAINTY

Our lives are by nature unpredictable, but we convince ourselves that we can plan for all contingencies. Most of us do everything in our power to insulate ourselves against sudden reversals of fortune. Climbing a high mountain crystallizes the uncertainty of life, its inherent peril, into a single effort that is far outside the bounds of safe conduct. Mountain climbing is a metaphor for our struggle towards higher meaning in a world that never offers straight answers. Merely existing above 8,000 metres (26,200 feet) is an achievement, at the whim of weather which could change to deadly at any second, where every move and even every thought is consequential. In 1963, Americans Thomas Hornbein and Willi Unsoeld completed the first ascent of Everest via the dangerous West Ridge (they were also the first to traverse the mountain). Hornbein later wrote about one of Barry Corbett's photographs of their ascent:

'His photo of two tiny figures, Willi Unsoeld and me, on the crest of the West Shoulder, dwarfed by the mountain soaring seductively above captures for me the essence of what our West Ridge adventure was about – savouring uncertainty.'[2]

This is sound advice with which to navigate a human life, subject to icefalls of outrageous fortune: savour that uncertainty, if you can. And you don't need to spend a night literally freezing your toes off at high altitude, as Willi Unsoeld did on the 1963 descent, to savour it. The few may suffer at high altitude to bring insights back down to sea level for the many. Recalling the aftermath of his Everest summit in a recent interview, Hornbein elaborated on the metaphorical meaning of the risky climb:

'After we got back to Seattle, Willi gave a talk about the trip. The audience mostly greeted us with adulation, but there were a few smart people who – even though we were back alive and well – thought we were really stupid and had no business trying to do the West Ridge. That's not uncommon in any endeavor where you venture into the unknown. You're taking risks and you don't know how it's going to turn out – that's a great metaphor for everything in life.'[3]

Mountain adventurers today explore not necessarily new terrain but new human relationships – with the self, with others, and with nature. In the following pages we will hear from several such present-day explorers and discover how and why they thrive in these environments. We'll also delve into the psychological benefits of mountains, and hear from conservationists, ecologists and botanists working in mountainous regions today. Before that, we'll rope up for a rappel into the world of high-altitude scientific research, focusing on mountains' wide-ranging impact on human health.

CHAPTER 2

PHYSICAL HEALTH AT HIGH ALTITUDE

~~~~~~~~~~

"Thousands of tired, nerve-
shaken, over-civilized
people are beginning to
find out that going to the
mountains is like going
home; that wildness is
a necessity..."

— John Muir

In myth and religion, mountains represent the holy simply because they rise above the world of flawed, earth-bound, suffering mortals. The Tibetan Buddhist legend of the kingdom of Shambhala – a paradise lost in a valley behind unscalable mountains, where people live free from strife and disease – may spring from a place informed partly by fact. Over the last decade or so, increasing numbers of studies have pinpointed the health benefits of being at higher altitude.

Does Mountain Life Increase Longevity?

For decades, scientists wondered at reports of extraordinarily long lifespans in Abkhazia (formerly in the Soviet Union and today a republic) in the Caucasus Mountains (pictured opposite). In the Soviet era, state doctors studied the population but results were inconclusive.[4] The reason for the region's large number of centenarians was probably due to a combination of factors, including unpolluted air and water; natural selection, abetted by the region's genetic isolation; Abkhazians' propensity for hard outdoor labour and daily exercise; even the local cultured buttermilk. But clearly the mountain setting was a major contributing factor, even if altitude alone was not producing the results.

And likewise, a study over 15 years on the adult populations of two lowland and one mountainous village in rural Greece found that residence in mountainous areas seems to have a protective effect over total mortality and heart mortality. The authors of the study suggested it might be due to increased physical exercise from walking on rugged terrain with less oxygen entering the bloodstream due to the altitude.[5]

Can Altitude Protect Against Metabolic Syndrome?

A recent study with concrete results linking higher altitude to improved human health came out of the University of Navarra in Pamplona, Spain. Researchers monitored a cohort of just under 7,000 healthy, well-educated Spanish adults over a period of 10 years, making note of their altitude of residence. The results were striking. Subjects in the highest category of altitude (456 metres/1,500 feet above sea level) showed a lower risk of developing metabolic syndrome than those living below 122 metres (400 feet). Metabolic syndrome – a catchall term for several conditions including obesity, high blood pressure and high cholesterol which increase the risk of stroke, heart disease and diabetes – is on the rise throughout the world.[6]

The study results suggest that living at a higher altitude (and thus having a lower amount of oxygen in the blood, among other factors) contributes to a lower incidence of obesity, to take just one example. Surprisingly, the study participants living at higher altitude exercised less on average than those at lower altitudes. They were also found to have a lower Body Mass Index (BMI) and ate more – they were 'more likely to snack between meals'.[7] After considering all the factors (including the aforementioned), the study concludes that 'to live at geographically higher altitude was directly associated with a lower risk of developing [metabolic syndrome].'

I asked one of the study authors, Pedro González-Muniesa, a lecturer at the University of Navarra, if he and his colleagues were surprised to find these results in subjects living at such a relatively low altitude (456 metres/1,500 feet). 'It is true that it is a very low altitude compared to other studies,' he said. Recent studies on human adaptations at high altitude examined subjects living much higher than this, including research from the University of Munich which detected a 'metabolic shift' in obese subjects, who lost significantly more weight at an altitude of 2,650 metres (8,700 feet), compared to low altitude.[8]

'In general, higher altitudes have been related to better glucose metabolism and lipid profile,' study co-author Prof. J. A. Martínez explained. 'Blood pressure in some studies is increased at higher altitudes; in our case it seems to be decreased although non-significant. Due to other studies that we have conducted, we believe that the extra exertion of breathing at higher altitude is one of the factors that leads to these positive effects.'

I asked González-Muniesa if, based on his findings, he would recommend we all move to 456 metres (1,500 feet) above sea level. He struck a cautious tone. 'What we would suggest to the general population is: eat well, be physically active, sleep enough and keep calm. If you have the possibility of living higher, it might be a good option, but it is too soon to make this assumption.' Co-author Amaya Lopez-Pascual is careful to point out: 'this is a preliminary result and future studies with longer follow-up periods, larger sample size and higher altitudes are needed...Moreover, our results need further validation in the general population.'

A Link Between Weight Loss and Altitude

Researchers have established a link between higher altitude and a reduction in obesity. A study of just under 10,000 American Army and Air Force personnel tracked the subjects over several years as they moved to bases at different altitudes. The personnel living above 1,950 metres (6,400 feet) turned out to be 40 per cent less likely to become obese than their colleagues below 975 metres (3,200 feet).

The higher caloric burn-rate of exercise at high altitude, where less oxygen is available to the lungs and bloodstream, may be the reason for the discrepancy. One other possibility is that people may experience a reduction in appetite at altitude, due to the resultant increase in levels of the hormone leptin, which could reduce the urge to overeat.[9]

FURTHER STUDIES LINKING HEALTH AND MOUNTAINS

- A University of Zurich study found that subjects' chances of dying from coronary heart disease decreased if they lived at high altitude (above 1,500 metres/4,900 feet).[10]

- Another study, from the Diabetes and Obesity Research Institute, Los Angeles, found that those living at higher altitudes have 'better glucose tolerance compared with those who live near sea level. There is also emerging evidence of the lower prevalence of both obesity and diabetes at higher altitudes.'[11]

- A University of Innsbruck paper reviewed a wide swath of current literature on the health consequences of living at altitude and concluded that 'residency at higher altitudes is associated with lower mortality from cardiovascular diseases, stroke and certain types of cancer.'[12]

The University of Innsbruck study places the number of people around the world living above 1,500 metres (4,900 feet) at approximately 400 million. Many millions more live in lower elevation mountain regions. Clearly, elevation can impact human health but the degrees of that impact need to be probed further. With so many millions living at high altitude, much remains to be learned. There is more on this in The Future for Mountain Research and Conservation chapter (see page 154).

The Beneficial Effects of a Natural Environment

The Japanese have long recognized the benefits of spending time in nature and the practice of *shinrin-yoku*, or 'forest bathing', is common in Japan. The country boasts many forest bathing centres where people immerse themselves in a forest environment in order to improve their wellbeing. It's not surprising that Japan is leading the way in research into the ways spending time in a natural environment can affect our health.

In a country-wide study testing 756 participants,[13] researchers found that those participants who spent time in a forest environment as compared to an urban area, showed the following effects:

- Lowered pulse rate

- Lowered blood pressure

- Reduced concentration of the stress hormone cortisol

- Increased parasympathetic nerve activity (the 'rest and digest' state – *see* page 32)

- Decreased sympathetic nerve activity (the 'fight or flight' state – *see* page 32)

- The results show the body experiences physiological relaxation when surrounded by nature, and what's more, these effects lasted for some weeks after the study

The wellbeing effects of spending time in nature are now the subject of research all over the world and it's clear that mountains can offer us these same effects, simply because they are natural places, untouched by urbanization.

IMPROVED IMMUNE FUNCTION AND SLEEP

More good news: moderate exercise in nature can cause the body to switch into a kind of deep but active relaxation or 'rest and digest' mode – contrary to the 'fight or flight' mode. The latter is a stress response where the body deems the immune system temporarily nonessential and curtails it. In a natural environment we consider safe, this 'rest and digest' mode directs more of our body's resources towards immunity.

Time in nature boosts the nervous system's parasympathetic activity, where our heartbeat moderates and our bodies repair muscle and send out calming hormones or neurotransmitters into the bloodstream. Ultimately all these recovery processes prepare us for better sleep by the end of the day.[14]

~~~~~~~~~

Prescribing Nature

Studies in environmental psychology make a clear connection between spending time in natural spaces such as mountains, and stress reduction. Some healthcare professionals now refer to contact with nature, and exercise in nature, as a 'therapeutic intervention' to enhance recovery from conditions related to stress, including some types of depression.[15] In Scotland – home to Ben Nevis, the highest mountain in the British Isles – doctors can now write 'nature' on a prescription. As part of a project undertaken by Shetland's National Health Service and The Royal Society for the Protection of Birds (RSPB) Scotland, doctors are encouraging patients to spend time in nature for the many proven benefits, including lower blood pressure and a reduction in the likelihood of stroke and heart disease. This prescription is also a drug-free (and cost-free) ticket to mental wellbeing.[16]

~~~~~~~~~

Mountain Exercise and Health

Perhaps one of the greatest benefits of the mountains to mankind is the opportunity for physical exercise. Most people, when living in or visiting the mountains, take part in some of the activities on offer, such as hiking, climbing or skiing. Research shows that certain environments might make us more likely to exercise by providing greater opportunities for such activities. It has been medically proven that those who take part in regular and moderate physical exercise have a reduced risk of illness and disease, as well as greater longevity.

- HIKING Even brisk walking can lower blood pressure and improve the performance of the heart and lungs, reducing the risk of many chronic illnesses such as type-2 diabetes, heart disease, stroke, asthmas and some forms of cancer. In fact, walking could be better for us than running or jogging. Researchers at the Lawrence Berkeley National Laboratory in California found that brisk walking reduces the risk of heart disease to a greater extent than running, if energy expenditure is the same for both activities.[17] Participants, aged between 18 and 80, were studied over a period of six years and researchers found that running reduced the risk of heart disease by 4.5 per cent, while walking reduced it by 9.3 per cent.

- CLIMBING uses all the major muscle groups in both the upper and lower body, exercising the back, abdominal and leg muscles as well as the fingers, shoulders and arms. Regular climbing increases stamina and endurance as well as muscle strength, and reaching and stretching for holds improves flexibility and agility.

- SKIING AND SNOWBOARDING These activities improve cardiovascular endurance and health, work all the major muscle groups, improve balance and agility, and strengthen bones and joints. The exercise releases endorphins into the blood, improving mood and leading to better sleep.

Exercising in Nature

It seems that exercising in nature can offer us advantages over exercising in a gym. One study found that when participants chose their own walking speed at which to exercise, those walking outdoors chose a faster speed than those indoors and, paradoxically, they felt that they had put in less effort on their walk.[18] When they were asked to walk using the same amount of effort indoors and outdoors, they walked at a faster rate outdoors, which suggests they may have found the exercise less demanding outside. Being in pleasant natural surroundings seems to make us less aware of physiological sensations, such as feeling tired, which allows us to exercise harder and for longer.

Hypoxia: A Problem and a Solution

Another burgeoning area of study focuses on a common affliction of mountaineers and many lowlanders who venture above about 2,500 metres (8,200 feet): hypoxia, a lack of oxygen reaching the body's tissues. The low barometric pressure at high altitude can cause hypoxia because in that environment, the body cannot process the normal amount of oxygen into the bloodstream, which causes shortness of breath. Hypoxia is not just a high-altitude phenomenon; it can occur whenever circulation to tissue or muscle is compromised, for example in asthma and anemia sufferers, and in some lung and heart diseases.

A recent field study in the Bolivian Andes monitored changes in the skeletal muscle of volunteers at 5,200 metres (17,100 feet) over a two-week period. Part of the AltitudeOmics Project – an ongoing high-altitude

research effort funded in part by the US Department of Defense and US National Institutes of Health – organizers flew volunteers from lowland regions of the US to Mount Chacaltaya in the Cordillera Real, central-west Bolivia.[19]

Catherine Le, a Ph.D graduate from the Cell and Molecular Biology Program at Colorado State University who now works as a scientist at Roche, lived on Chacaltaya for the duration of the study, and co-authored the resulting paper. 'This was an immense study; one of the major strengths of this project was that it was an eclectic group of individuals, who brought in several areas of expertise…it was a tremendous opportunity for me to learn and discuss the complex impacts of high altitude and hypoxia at the physiological level and down to the genetic level with experts from fields outside of mitochondrial research.

'I am excited to be part of scientific work that will expand on our current understanding of the molecular mechanisms of hypoxia adaptation in skeletal muscle mitochondria. This research can help us to develop new ideas on how to treat patients with hypoxia-related diseases.'

How Our Bodies 'Remodel' at Altitude

Adam Chicco, an associate professor in Colorado State's Department of Biomedical Sciences and lead author of the paper,[20] explained the background to the study: 'Physiologically, spending time at high altitude can be stressful due to hypoxemia (lower oxygen levels in our blood), as well as cold exposure, solar radiation and low humidity. Modern technology can largely protect us from these challenges now, but most who spend days or more at habitable altitudes will at least partially endure and ultimately adjust to these stressors. This process, known as high-altitude acclimatization, involves both transient and sustained changes in nearly all body systems, particularly those that control the uptake and utilization of oxygen.'

Chicco put his team's role into context: 'Our study focused on the adjustments that occur in skeletal muscle of young adults…We found that adjustments favour a reduced energy cost of daily activity and improvements in the efficiency of energy production of available fuels (fats, proteins and carbohydrates). Over time, this comes at the expense of lower muscle mass and perhaps reduced exercise capacity, but this "remodeling" of our physiology allows us to thrive in the new environment.'

This 'remodelling' that Chicco and colleagues observed could prove to have applications far beyond its high-altitude setting. 'Interestingly, hypoxemia also occurs in debilitating heart and lung diseases, and is thought to trigger processes which impair our ability to perform our routine daily activities,' Chicco explained. 'Understanding how healthy individuals respond to low oxygen conditions at high altitude can help us to distinguish the adaptive (healthy) from maladaptive (unhealthy) changes in disease states, perhaps leading to better directed therapies which target the damaging but not the beneficial processes, to improve disease outcomes.'

~~~~~~~~~~

A Scientist Finds Solitude and Peace

I asked Adam Chicco (*see* page 36) for his take on the greater meaning of mountains in his life and in the context of the study carried out in the Bolivian Andes (pictured opposite). 'The study participants and scientists were delighted to be part of the project, and even more excited about spending time in the Bolivian Andes,' he said. 'Such is the case for all high-altitude studies I've seen or been involved with – it's never difficult to sign up volunteers. I suppose our attraction to high mountain places derives from a primal desire for safety and advantage over competitors, looking down on vast, imposing terrain from a relative position of freedom and strength. In a more modern sense, the majesty of mountains inspires us to explore and challenge ourselves, perhaps to capture some of their grandeur or discover it in ourselves. Indeed, I think the solitude and peace earned by reaching these places is central to their attraction and the contemplative experience we often find there.'

~~~~~~~~~~

Medicine from the Mountains

Many mountain ranges have unique ecosystems which are largely unaffected by mankind as they are often inhospitable places. These ecosystems contain many endemic plants, often highly evolved to thrive in their unique surroundings. Certain species are being 'discovered' by medicinal science for their possible use in a wide range of treatments, but in many cases they have been used in the traditional medicine of the local population for many generations.

The world's highest mountain system, the Himalayas, rises between the Tibetan Plateau and the Indian subcontinent. Here, more than 110 peaks reach elevations of at least 7,300 metres (24,000 feet) above sea level. Known as earth's 'Third Pole', the Himalayas comprise many different ecosystems and climatic zones which host unrivalled biodiversity, including many medicinal plants. Here's a short list of three such species and their purported uses.

Picrorhiza scrophulariiflora (Pennell)

This herbaceous plant is found mainly on rocky terrain in the sub-alpine and alpine zones of the eastern Himalayas of India, China and Nepal. In traditional Chinese and Tibetan medicine, pennell root is used to treat fever, liver disorders, asthma and jaundice. Scientific research suggests it is effective at enhancing human immune system function.

Prunella vulgaris (Self-heal)

This perennial herb is plentiful in the Kashmir Himalaya, where it is traditionally used as an astringent and in the treatment of fever and ulcers. It is also used to treat liver ailments, pulmonary disease and vertigo, and as an anti-parasitic and an anti-rheumatic agent. It has also displayed anti-viral properties, and may help to inhibit anaphylactic shock and other allergic reactions.

Artemisia indica Willd (Mugwort)

Mugwort (pictured right) is an aromatic herb in the Asteraceae family, which is native to the Uttarakhand (northern Indian) Himalayan region. Traditionally it is used to relieve headache and fever. Leaves are used to relieve skin itching and minor irritations. It has also displayed insecticide properties. Pharmacological uses of the root extracts include the reduction of post-operative blood loss and inflammation. Some derivatives of the plant are also sometimes used to treat malaria.[21]

CHAPTER 3

THE PSYCHOLOGICAL BENEFITS OF MOUNTAINS

~~~~~~~~~

"No matter how sophisticated you may be, a large granite mountain cannot be denied – it speaks in silence to the very core of your being."

— Ansel Adams

We've seen how mountains can benefit our physical health, but what about our mental health? This section explores the psychological and emotional benefits mountains can offer us, from allowing us to experience awe, embrace discomfort and regain contact with nature, to providing us with sacred symbols for our spiritual wellbeing.

The Sublime and Its Benefits

The high mountain landscape may be contemplative and beautiful but is also a little terrifying – or 'sublime' as defined by Irish-born philosopher Edmund Burke (1729–1797). In his influential 1757 essay *A Philosophical Enquiry into the Origin of Our Ideas of the Sublime and Beautiful*, Burke contended that the sublime is triggered in nature by 'greatness of dimension' or 'looking down from a precipice'. In a high mountain range, the human eye can't 'perceive the bounds', and this ushers in the 'strongest emotion which the mind is capable of feeling.' Burke adds: 'Infinity has a tendency to fill the mind with that sort of delightful horror, which is the most genuine effect, and truest test of the sublime.'

Art, the Sublime and Its Uses

This notion of the sublime became a moody blueprint for Romantic literature and art, where certain nature scenes embodied human turmoil or aspirations (as seen in the work of the English Romantic poets) or reflected our various understandings of the divine and nature (as seen in the Romantic school of landscape painting led by German Caspar David Friedrich). Two of Friedrich's paintings – *The Cross in the Mountains* (also known as *The Tetschen Altar*, painted in 1808) and *Morning in the Riesengebirge* (painted in 1810–11) – set the Crucifixion in the midst of mountainous wilderness. This unorthodox placement of such an omnipresent symbol depicts nature as transformative – overpowering our suffering even while it offers no comfort.

There may not be a work that more immediately denotes the sublime and the elemental forces of mountains than English painter Turner's 1810 *The Fall of an Avalanche in the Grisons*. This oil puts the viewer in the path of the snowslide, reminding us that nature can crush in an instant. Rather than a vista meant to inspire lofty thoughts, it offers an unforgettable aspect of the mountain's true character. This isn't scenery: it is primordial savagery.

In light of these examples, one might reasonably ask: what is the use of the sublime, this strongest of emotions? If we can harness the emotions inspired by earth's wildest landscapes and mould them into something that is beneficial to us, then the process certainly has its uses. And a study on aspects of the sublime is doing just that.

WHY EXPERIENCING AWE IS GOOD FOR US

Melanie Rudd grew up within sight of Mount Rainier in Washington State. Now an Assistant Professor of Marketing at the University of Houston, she specializes in studies of awe. (One of the definitions of awe in the *Oxford English Dictionary* is 'the feeling of solemn and reverential wonder, tingled with latent fear, inspired by what is terribly sublime and majestic in nature.') Most of us would probably never suspect that awe could actually open up our shuttered creativity – and mountain scenery, which serves up all-you-can-eat portions of awe, is the key, according to Rudd and her colleagues.

'I've always been a mountain person in general,' said Rudd. 'My dad was a mountain climber: when I was growing up he climbed all the major peaks in the Pacific Northwest. As a little kid I was playing with crampons on, walking around in the backyard. I've always had that connection to mountains, so when I started doing research on awe, one of the obvious stimuli to use was mountains. Even though I grew up seeing Mount Rainier – not every day, it depended on the weather –

the mountain would provide me with a regular dose of awe throughout the day. And now that I live in Texas and don't see it as often, the mountain elicits even more awe whenever I go back home for a visit. So mountains were one of the first things my mind went to when I started to think about awe in everyday life.'

Time, Awe and Nature

'I took a class when I was a Ph.D student, on culture and emotion,' Rudd continued, 'and I started to encounter some older, more philosophical writings on the emotion of awe (at the time, there really wasn't much empirical research on awe). And every once in a while, I would read something about how time seems to move differently when you're in awe – that there might be some distortion of people's perception of time such that time felt more expansive. I started to wonder if that was real: do people really feel that way and can it influence their downstream decision-making, if they experience awe?

'In my life, I always seem to feel like I have no time. So in some ways this was kind of a self-interested research question: "How can consumers feel like they have more time?" People often study what they're the worst at. For me, that's having time as a resource. I've always had that in the back of my mind. And this idea of studying awe and time fitted well with my natural interest in the outdoors, as awe and nature are strongly linked. One of the things that's special about awe as an emotion is that it's very present-orienting. You really can't be focused on the past or the future while you're experiencing awe. It really sucks you into the moment. And that in part is what drives this time-perception effect and makes people feel that time is more expansive. Moreover, awe's ability to expand perceptions of time leads you to be more willing to spend time helping other people, and makes you more strongly desire experiences, as opposed to material goods – which is also a plus for your wellbeing.'

CAN MOUNTAINS INSPIRE CREATIVITY?

Rudd is lead author of a 2018 study in the *Journal of Marketing Research*[22] that examines what motivates people's willingness to learn and to create, specifically to engage in 'experiential creation', including assembling the hiker's venerable hunger-slaying confection, trail mix, which it turns out, can fuel not just your scramble up into the alpine, but also benchmark your creativity. Rudd explained as follows: 'Experiential creation can be any activity where you play a direct role in the outcome as a creator. You're not playing a passive role and watching someone else create. You're not pushing a button and something pops out, created. You're actually part of the experience. There's a lot of research that shows how people get benefits from creating – not only because we value the things we create, but the act itself is very fulfilling.'

One study examined subjects in the Swiss Alps: one group at the bottom of a mountain in a non-awe-inspiring environment, and the other at the top in a high-awe setting. Rudd explained: 'We measured the participants' desire to create by having them choose either a pre-made trail mix, or make their own – trying to determine if those at the top of the mountain where it was more awe-inspiring would choose to create their own assortment (as opposed to those down in the parking lot by the beginning of the cable car line). We also gave them the opportunity to learn by offering both groups an educational brochure about hiking. So we measured both of those factors and saw that the people at the top were more open to learning and that this greater openness to learning made them more likely to create their own trail mix.'

The fact that the study participants in the grip of awe wanted to take the time to create something, even if it was pretty mundane stuff (cranberries, apricots, hazelnuts, cashews and raisins: the ingredients the study organizers offered them for create-your-own trail mix), and learn more about their surroundings, was significant. And it was not the only upside to the high-mountain group's experience.

'We used mountains in another experiment,' Rudd continued, 'where we randomly showed people one of three ads for a fake ski resort (which they didn't know was fake) – one with an awe-inspiring picture of a mountain; another with a skier doing an exciting jump; and then a neutral picture of skis on a ski rack. And here we again saw [in the

reaction to the mountain picture], a greater openness to learning and greater desire to create...Awe can make you more open to learning and bite you with the creativity bug, both of which are beneficial to humans but are also things we don't experience frequently enough. Growing up, I liked to create, even though I was not a very good artist. As I get older, I find I don't quite feel the same desire on a regular basis, so one of the things I thought would be important was to see if I could link awe into that general idea – to see if there was a way to get people to have a stronger desire to create.'

Rudd and her co-authors tie the creative impulse to what they call 'accommodation'. That is, when we experience an awe-inspiring mountain view, for example, it may be difficult for us to immediately understand or summarize it. Therefore, we may feel our current self-knowledge or belief structures need to be overhauled in some way. We thus 'accommodate' the awe experience into our everyday life. And this action subsequently encourages various forms of creativity.

Awe Rewires Us to Create

'Generally when you're experiencing positive emotions, you tend to rely on a lot of your existing knowledge,' said Rudd. 'You're like, "I'm feeling good and I'm confident in my existing knowledge." But something about awe is different: it makes you feel like you need to adjust your way of thinking, but not in a negative way. Most of the time, the idea of changing how you think is scary and threatening. But when you're experiencing awe, it's a positive feeling, and it reassures you that this is not a dangerous situation – this is a safe environment, so it's OK to open your mind and think. When we're feeling this way, our desire to create just shoots up.'

If we experience awe in a mountain setting for the first time, Rudd explained, 'we have a hard time fully grasping this different thing, and this is especially true for people who didn't grow up around mountains. A lot is happening in our brains – a lot of cognitive effort and emotion, a lot of different activation – when humans open themselves up to learning in this pure way. There's something special about awe that does this. There's a lot of research into different emotions serving different evolutionary functions – what purpose would this emotion serve? Why do we feel this way? And a lot of research on awe has indicated that it changes the way we think. And that is valuable from a survival perspective – that is what awe's true function is – not just to make you feel good, but to change your brain.'

Could this awe-activated brain rewiring also be the key to Rudd's premise that awe makes us feel we have more time available to us? 'Time and wellbeing are very much related,' she said. 'And the reason why expanding your perception of time seems to be beneficial is that humans tend to feel that we have far less time than we actually do. Our perception is often that our time is really constrained when it isn't. If you look at how much free time people had in the past – we have way more free time now, and we're able to do the same tasks much more quickly. By these metrics we should feel that we all have tons of time. But it's almost worse than ever before, how time-pressed we feel. So expanding your perception of time is a way of hopefully better calibrating your time perception, which is important because feeling that you're in control of your life and have some kind of control over time – that it's not spinning out of control or slipping away – is very much tied to your wellbeing.'

Chasing Awe

So if we're feeling slammed by all the demands of family and work, should we drop everything and climb a mountain, seeking out the highest peak within a reasonable distance, so we might better manage our time? 'One misperception of awe is that sometimes people think it has to be this extreme experience,' Rudd said. 'They might not realize how easy it is to experience awe if you make a conscious effort to do so. Just like we can feel a little bit of happiness or a lot of happiness in an experience, you can feel a little bit of awe or a lot of awe depending on the experience too.

'So even though actually being in the Swiss Alps would be more awe-inspiring than a postcard of the Swiss Alps, you can still get it from the latter, just to a lesser extent. Personally, I get more awe from actually being on Mount Rainier and hiking around with my park ranger friends. There are degrees of awe, but people tend to forget that smaller doses of awe are still beneficial. If you drive through a national park, that's still beneficial, though perhaps not to the same degree as hiking up the mountain trails. But I'll take whatever awe I can get.'

Nature Boosts Creative Problem Solving

With both adults and children spending more and more time interacting with technology, our skills in selective attention, problem solving and multitasking are being used to the full. Research suggests that exposure to nature can help boost these functions and restore our attentional capabilities. However, it's important to leave the technology at home. In one study, participants spent four days hiking in the wilderness, without any technological devices. At the end of the four days, their performance on creative problem-solving tasks rose by a massive 50 per cent.[23]

Mountains as Sacred Symbols

The feeling of awe that mountains unlock is just one aspect of their totemic power. Certain mountains hold many layers of meaning, encompassing the worlds of art and religion, and thousands of years in a country's history. Both Buddhists and followers of Shinto hold sacred Mount Fuji (pictured opposite) – a 3,776-metre (12,400-foot) volcano about 100km (62 miles) southwest of Tokyo, Japan. It is the site of many shrines to Shinto – the ancient polytheistic folk religion of Japan – placed for pilgrims as waypoints to guide them in the warmer months up to the summit crater, which is believed to be the home or resting place of the Shinto deity associated with the volcano. For centuries, pilgrims have performed a ritual *ohachimeguri* or 'walk around the bowl' as a way of paying respect to the slumbering demigod. For many centuries, paying respect was a good idea: Fuji erupted at least 16 times between 781 and the most recent eruption in 1707.

Hokusai Frames Fuji

The prolific Japanese artist and print-maker Katsushika Hokusai (1760–1849) focused his work in the last decades of his life on various views of the mountain, framing it from unlikely viewpoints to accentuate its enduring symmetry in the face of changeable phenomena. As Fuji was a Shinto *kami*, a place inhabited by a spirit or spirits able to guide and counsel believers, this aura was (and still may be today for many) inseparable from the volcano. Nothing sums up its power better than one of the most influential and reproduced works of world art, Hokusai's wood-block print *The Great Wave Off Kanagawa*, from his 1830–35 series *Thirty-Six Views of Mount Fuji*. Here the serene mountain is framed by a curling wave in the foreground; half-obscured under the wave's merciless force, rows of tiny, faceless fishermen in two boats are about to be upended.

The Celestial Volcano

Fuji permeates Japanese culture to a degree unmatched by any mountain in any other country, apart from Everest. And since Everest straddles the border of Tibet and Nepal and is just one sacred peak among many in the Himalaya, Fuji by contrast becomes even more singular. Fuji is the archetypal mountain that engenders mythologies and belief systems which join the earth to the celestial and spur humanity to seek spiritual meaning and guidance in nature.

Fuji's conical shape is pleasing to our sense of symmetry but is by no means assured, for if the volcano again erupts, the force of the eruption and the amount of material ejected could severely alter the cone's shape. We think of mountains as eternal and fixed, but relatively young mountain ranges such as the Himalaya are still growing higher, a few centimetres every year, due to continuous tectonic forces. And active volcanoes such as Fuji exist in a state of flux and upheaval much more evident than the equally transformative but less cataclysmic mountain-making forces of tectonics and erosion.

Perhaps the pilgrims (and pilgrim-tourists) who climb Fuji every summer (it is not a technical climb) are doing so partly out of reverence to the kami or spirit resident in the mountain – if it is appeased, it will be less inclined to awaken in a foul mood. As American philosopher James Heisig observed of the animistic beliefs from which Fuji is inseparable, 'The Gods of Shinto are the life of the natural world in all its rich variety. The sacred does not lie outside of life but is one with it.'

Cherishing the Discomfort of Mountains

He's paddled, trekked and climbed in the world's most desolate and far-flung places – from Borneo's northern coast to the Arabian Peninsula's Empty Quarter to Axel Heiberg Island's towering gypsum cliffs – but Bruce Kirkby, the British Columbia-based adventure guide, writer and photographer, believes adventure can just as easily happen outside his back door.

After moving to Kimberley, a former mining town in southeastern British Columbia between the Rocky Mountains and the Purcell Range, Kirkby, his wife Christine and their infant son Bodi in a backpack, walked into the bush for a week-and-a-half-long trek along narrow game trails, overgrown logging roads and steep ridges, into the heart of the Purcells. 'My house is on the edge of the forest and we walked out our back door with ten days of food, straight into the forest. And kept walking. At one point we were going over Rose Pass and Bodi was complaining and crying and it was sleeting and snowing. We got to a cabin and realized we had put plastic bags over Bodi's socks, but then his shoes on over them: the way the plastic bags were positioned, they'd been catching all the water from his rain suit. So his shoes were full of ice water. And he did *not* like that...but then we sparked up a fire in the cabin. We had ten packets of Quaker instant oatmeal and I was pretty hungry. My wife said, 'We're going to give Bodi everything he needs until he stops eating!' Well, he ate six of those things himself and we got two each....So he wasn't injured from the cold, and the discomfort passed and what matters when you're 16 months old is just being with your parents – that undistracted time. And subconsciously our kids became comfortable with being outdoors.'

This anecdote serves to highlight Kirkby's belief in spontaneous, off-grid, off-road travel, often with family in tow, which avoids creature comforts and predictability. In his books, articles and speaking engagements, Kirkby offers a celebration of discomfort and an examination of why it can be a good thing.

The Scandinavians' Respect for Nature

The Scandinavians have long acknowledged the importance of spending time outdoors in nature, and even have a word for it. *Friluftsliv* literally translates as 'open-air living' and was popularized in the 1850s by Henrik Ibsen, the Norwegian playwright, who used the word to describe the value of spending time in rural locations for both emotional and physical wellbeing.

The concept of *friluftsliv* has been popular in Norway, Denmark and Sweden for over a century and employers recognize its importance: many businesses give their employees afternoons off to cycle or hike in the countryside. They see it as a way to improve the wellbeing of their employees and increase the productivity of the business.

A Mountain Epiphany

To trace the beginning of his life outdoors in rugged places, Bruce Kirkby (*see* page 55) describes a mountain epiphany of sorts that occurred when he was a young teenager. 'I grew up in Toronto and my dad was a nuclear physicist and he had a conference in Victoria [British Columbia]. So we all went out to the coast. We rented something called a Rent-a-Wreck car and drove into the Okanagan Valley. It was the total family vacation, three kids packed in a station wagon.

'When we got to Revelstoke it was puking rain and I thought we might be able to force my dad to get a motel tonight and not camp. It's absolutely sheeting down, you know? But my Dad was like, "Of course we've got to camp!" So we drove up to Glacier National Park. It's still puking with rain. We set up our Egyptian cotton pup tent and my mom and brother and sister were in the big tent. The next morning I unzipped the door, it had rained all night, and in front of me was the Illecillewaet Glacier and *big* mountains. I am convinced that that moment, that ten seconds, changed the course of my life. I came back out here 15 years later, searching for that. That was the way in for me.'

This 'way in' provided by that first view of mountains led Kirkby to take up adventure guiding. 'The mountains are a great teacher and you apprentice in them: you think you know a ton when you're 20 years old. And then you realize you knew nothing, but slowly, bit by bit, you learn.' Kirkby describes taking clients from all walks of life, and often business people, on week-long or longer paddling trips in the Canadian north. 'Everyone comes with all their worries, no matter what it is – their mortgage, work, everything they feel they need to deal with – ten days later when we get to the end of the trip, that stuff just doesn't matter. Being in the wilderness has a positive effect on people in that it's such an intangible thing. Why? Obviously we live in such an urbanized time

and wilderness is a need of humans. We live such compartmentalized, individualized, isolated lives and everyone's got their earbuds in. When we fly in a plane, where we used to all watch the same movie, now everyone watches their own movie. We all strive for comfort – but comfort never brings true happiness. I'm more comfortable with discomfort.

'That's a life idea of mine – there's something weird in how we are getting ourselves programmed to seek comfort and I think it's because we've got so many little stressors – phones beeping – so we want anything to just calm the nerves. We get into a short-sighted search for comfort. Everything that's good in your life – your marriage, your kids, your trips – it isn't comfortable but it's freaking great. Mountains and wilderness in general are restorative for what's inside everyone. In the mountains there's no limit on how far you can push yourself: it's a scale that has no end. You can be as challenged as you want. You don't master it, like being able to ride a Century [cycling 161km/100 miles or more in a day]. You can shave off the time of a marathon by a little, but you can go on a mountain and be gripped any day you want to.'

A Human Need for the Wild

'I think nearly all humans have a natural love for the outdoors, for wild things,' he said. 'We see a baby tiger being held in its mom's teeth, we see some extraordinary mountain scene, and it resonates with us. But an increasing number of us, even though we love wild places, have lost the skill of how to really be in them and receive the more subtle but perhaps deeper rewards they can give us. So we take in the *National Geographic* highlight reels and that type of thing. But if you took an average person out to sit in a city park all day, they'd say, "This is boring!". The mountains are an easy way in; they are so in-your-face. They're so easy to love. They're like the baby tiger. I think that's so important right now because we see so much urbanization and sequestration from wild places.'

Kirkby is right. As a species we're rapidly evolving into dedicated city dwellers – recent numbers from a study conducted by the United Nations leave no doubt about it. The global population living in urban areas grew from 751 million in 1950 to over 4 billion in 2018. Fifty-five per cent of earth's population lives in cities today, and by 2050 the UN projects this proportion to increase to sixty-eight per cent.

And yet, as Kirkby suggests, something in us nonetheless rejects being crowded into grids, no matter how comfortable, convenient and mostly predictable our lives might be within them. Perhaps we see a high mountain range stretching off into an apparent infinity of rock, snow and ice as a symbol of our salvation from the ever-mounting costs of both industrial and technological progress.

~~~~~~~~~

Nature and the 'Reinvented Self'

In the Canadian province of Alberta, where the Prairies swell into the foothills and then the Rocky Mountains, Mount Royal University and the province's Environment and Parks ministry recently studied the effect of nature experiences on adults with disabilities and their caregivers.

The project's researchers designed therapeutic programs in the mountains, including day trips and prolonged trips to the backcountry, and interviewed or surveyed the participants before and after. Results were overwhelmingly positive. The researchers pinpointed three main themes in participant accounts of their experiences during the program: Sensory Activation, Reimagined Social Relations and Reinvented Self. Immersion in nature and the mountains lessened participants' depression and also brightened their outlook on their physical health. In interviews, participants singled out certain sensory experiences, including feeling soothed by the sound of running water. They also reported that their social relationships or their impression of them improved – specifically in the areas of love and friendship – as well as their feelings of community and empathy.[24]

~~~~~~~~~

Developing Respect for Mountains

With only about 12,000 permanent residents but an estimated 3 million annual visitors, Whistler in British Columbia (pictured opposite) is a purpose-built mountain town overshadowed by the side-by-side peaks of Whistler and Blackcomb in the Fitzsimmons Range of the Coast Mountains. Dating back at least a century, the name 'Whistler' refers to the slope-side colonies of whistling marmots (Marmota caligata cascadensis). The resort, which includes the twin mountains and over 8,000 acres of slopes, three glaciers and 16 alpine bowls, boasts the two longest vertical drops of any ski region in North America.

Olympic snowboarder Dominique Vallée moved to Whistler from Quebec when she was 18. Showing promise as a young teenager after switching from skis to snowboard, she exchanged her home hills for higher mountains (Vallée was born in Montreal and learned to snowboard at the family chalet in western Quebec's Laurentians, an ancient Precambrian range with peaks no higher than 1,190 metres/ 3,900 feet). Her career would take her to the 2006 Olympic Games in Turin, competing in both halfpipe and snowboard-cross. She won World Cup bronze in halfpipe, and was the four-time halfpipe Canadian national champion. Under the pressure of international competition, Vallée would find solace on mountains all over the world: 'When you get to the event, whether it's training or contest day, that's a very small zone of the mountain. You'd do your halfpipe run and get in the gates, and everyone's nervous, you'd do your run and maybe it didn't go according to plan, you could just go and see the mountains and give yourself a reality check that there are bigger things in the world.'

'The Mountain Can Eat You Up'

She retired from competition in 2010 and for the next six years, explored mountains around the world, snowboarding for sponsored film shoots. This phase of her career was a more immersive mountain experience and non-competitive, but wasn't without its own pressures and dangers. 'We'd have a week or ten days to get all these shots for a magazine or

a film,' Vallée explained. 'This was really different from competing...you were there to just milk it and throw your body off cliffs. When you're trying to asses a line, or climbing up a sketchy mountain, or you're on a peak and you're going to drop a cornice, things can happen in seconds. You have to be so present. What you're having for dinner that night, or what you did yesterday – you can't think about that. There's no space in your brain.'

Vallée described a film shoot near Tailgate, in central Alaska: 'In Alaska you feel like the tiniest speck in the world, you could get swallowed up in a crater or fall through an ice sheet, and no one will find you.' In big mountain snowboard or ski shoots, where sponsors and filmmakers require athletes to go ever higher in search of impossible lines, the mission seldom goes according to plan. 'You think it's going to be an easy hike with good snowpack,' she added, 'but then you realize it's pointy rocks with ice and you should be wearing crampons and using ice picks, but it's too far to go back. So you just scramble up and glue yourself onto the mountain. There's no room for mistakes. I had a friend fall into an ice cavern where our radio couldn't connect and that person could have died in front of me. What do you take away from that? Huge respect for the mountain. When you lose that respect, things usually go wrong. But even if you have all the experience in the world, the mountain can still eat you up.'

Regaining Contact with Nature

After a career in competitive snowboarding, and then as a sponsored athlete on demanding and dangerous shoots, Vallée decided she needed to transition into a second career. Having called on Traditional Chinese Medicine (TCM) to help boost her immune system in her competitive days, she began training to be a doctor of TCM while winding down her sponsored snowboard shoots, and was certified in 2017. When talking about her

TCM practice, Vallée mentions the ancient Chinese physician Qibo, acknowledged as one of the founders of Chinese medicine whose therapies (or at least those attributed to him by later writers) laid groundwork not just for acupuncture but also for nature therapy. The latter is an exploding health discipline, as researchers continue to discover in study after study that exposure to daily prolonged doses of nature can result in a host of positive effects, from lowering blood pressure and stress to increasing our sense of contentment and happiness, and our ability to focus (*see* page 68).[25]

According to Vallée, 'When we lose our contact with nature, it starts to disintegrate the wheel of health. If Qibo were here today, he'd be traumatized. No one is really present anymore. We're running ourselves into the ground. Our brains and bodies can't adapt as fast as technology is evolving. If we look at our parents, what we do in ten minutes is what they used to do in about a week of work. If you spend more time outside, you become more mentally at ease. You have better sleep. There's a lot of stress and anxiety in a mountain community like Whistler, too, but by just being in nature, everyone must slow down. When you go camping in the mountains, by day two, it's like someone stuck a tranquilizing dart in your butt – your nervous system slows down and relaxes. And this should be your normal state.'

Mountain Exercise and Mental Wellbeing

On top of the physical benefits of exercising in the mountains (*see* page 34), it seems our mental health can benefit too. Exercising in a natural environment improves self-esteem, boosts confidence, boosts creativity, helps concentration and focus, and improves mood, reducing tension, anger and depression.

The stresses of urban living – constant noise and too many things vying for our attention at any one time – lead to 'brain fatigue', when we feel distracted and find it difficult to concentrate. The results of a recent study in Edinburgh, Scotland, have shown that walking through a green space can have a calming effect on our brains.[26] Lightweight brain-scanners were fitted to the heads of 12 people as they walked through the city. The results showed that while busy, built-up areas induced frustration and irritation in the participants, green areas and parks caused the brain to calm and become more meditative, reducing brain fatigue. While natural settings hold our attention, they are not so demanding they don't allow scope for reflection. They allow our brains to relax for a while, allowing our minds to wander along with our bodies.

~~~~~~~~

Walking Can Treat Depression

The simple act of getting out for a walk has been shown to be almost as effective as anti-depressant drugs in the treatment of depression. A four-month study found that 45 per cent of patients diagnosed with major depression were no longer depressed after walking three times a week in a supervised group setting. This compares to 47 per cent of those who were prescribed anti-depressants during the same period.[27]

Only 40 per cent of those who exercised alone achieved remission, proving that exercising with others can have a much greater impact as it provides the opportunity to build relationships and social networks and to talk through problems.

Climbing for Mental Health

Climbing improves your self esteem and self awareness. It requires a lot of problem solving, concentration and focus, so it helps sharpen your brain. It relieves stress as it allows you to forget everyday worries as you focus on the climb. And if you make it to the top, it can also offer a great sense of achievement. Many climbers say they participate in the activity for the social aspect. You develop strong bonds with your climbing partners because of the trust involved, and through the shared challenges and experiences.

Skiing and Snowboarding

These relatively fast-paced sports force us to make strategic decisions quickly, choosing the best routes and remaining aware of other skiers or trees around us, which improves our concentration and cognitive capacity. This clearer thinking makes regular skiiers more likely to be better learners in other areas of life, and could protect against mental decline in old age.

~~~~~~~~

Sharpening the Mind

Can mountain-hiking also sharpen your mind? Research not only supports this claim but suggests that exercise can *grow your brain*. A protein known as BDNF (Brain-Derived Neurotrophic Factor) develops nerves in the brain associated with learning and memory in infants.

As we age, our BDNF levels tend to decrease. But evidence is mounting that cardiovascular exercise such as hiking increases BDNF levels and thus improves overall cognitive function, including memory. By producing more BDNF, we strengthen the brain's nerve structures and promote the storage of new information.[28]

CHAPTER 4

A MOUNTAIN WAY OF LIFE

〜〜〜〜〜〜〜〜

"Mountains are the
beginning and the end
of all natural scenery."

— John Ruskin

John Muir Tramps West

In the second half of the 19th century, an idea began to emerge, particularly in the United States, that mountain landscapes did not function merely as holy realms or picturesque eyries – but also as places that needed protection from mining, logging and agriculture. Extractive industries were beginning to scar heavily the landscape that Europeans had found largely pristine when they began settling North America in great numbers, marching steadily west of the Mississippi River along the Oregon Trail. This shift towards the movements we now recognize as environmentalism and conservation started, one could argue, in the mountains of California.

John Muir, the father of the US National Parks movement and founder of the Sierra Club, was born in Dunbar, Scotland, in 1838; he and his family emigrated to Wisconsin when he was 11. Entering his twenties, Muir was a university drop-out of modest means who, with his overgrown beard, rustic clothing and peripatetic ways, would have looked and felt incongruous in the average Gilded Age drawing room. For several years after leaving the University of Wisconsin without a degree (though he excelled in the subjects of botany and geology), he rambled around eastern North America, taking work where he could find it.

During the American Civil War, Muir relocated to Canada to work in a mill in Meaford, Ontario, then moved back to the US after the war to work as a machinist in Indianapolis, Indiana, where he temporarily blinded himself in an accident. After recovering, Muir began to travel even more, aimlessly but no less courageously, mostly alone and on foot from the Midwest, through a lawless post-war South, to the Gulf of Mexico. He later wrote in a notebook about this time, 'I was tormented with soul hunger...I began to doubt whether I was fully born. I was on the world...but was I in it?'

He yearned to pursue botany in the footsteps of his hero, the German naturalist Alexander von Humboldt who had explored the Andes at the turn of the 19th century, collecting plant specimens, filling countless notebooks with measurements and notes and climbing the Ecuadorian stratovolcano Chimborazo, then thought to be earth's highest mountain. 'How intensely I desire to be a Humboldt,' Muir wrote in a letter.[29]

On the side of the volcano, Humboldt observed zones of vegetation succeeding one another, from the subtropical at the bottom to the

Arctic-like barrens at the top; here he suddenly understood how to organize plant-life based upon variables of climate and location. This notion of stacked ecosystems, all immediately dependent on one another, would prove influential to Muir and other early environmentalists and biologists, as well as to the study of ecology today. Chimborazo's towering position in orology is assured, even if – at 6,268 metres (20,600 feet) to Everest's 8,848 metres (29,000 feet) – it would eventually prove to be far from the highest mountain in the world. And yet due to its proximity to the Equator and earth's paunchy-sphere shape, Chimborazo is in one sense the highest – its summit is nearest to outer space if its height is calculated not from sea level, but from the centre of the earth.

Unlike Humboldt (who died in his 90th year in 1859, having written more than 30 books), Muir was not born into the Prussian aristocracy and could not fund his own scientific expeditions. Muir could not even afford the passage to South America and found himself stalled in Cuba, recovering from a spell of malaria picked up while botanizing in the swamps of Florida. Eventually he made his way west to San Francisco, then a small city growing fast on the heels of the Gold Rush. Muir disliked cities and wasted no time heading inland in what became a pattern that would last his lifetime – making a beeline for the nearest mountains, in the opposite direction of the crowds. Instead of following Humboldt to the Andes, the young Muir blazed his own path towards the Sierra Nevada mountains, which he would later refer to as the 'Range of Light'.

SAVING THE SIERRA

The Sierra Nevada (pictured) is a major range in eastern California which stretches more than 400km (250 miles) north from the Mojave Desert and spans about 130km

(80 miles) at its widest point. Its highest peak is Mount Whitney (4,418 metres/14,500 feet). Much of the high Sierra is snow-covered year round but due to the dramatic valleys carved by glaciers, and the variety of elevation and good soil quality, the range hosts extraordinary biodiversity.

Just one example is earth's largest tree, the giant sequoia (*Sequoiadendron giganteum*), arrayed in three groves today protected inside Sequoia National Park. A sequoia can grow over 90 metres (295 feet) tall with a girth of up to 45 metres (148 feet), and live for more than 3,000 years. Muir called giant sequoias 'the noblest conifers in the world...a monarch of monarchs' and was one of the first to study, sketch and publish articles about the trees. US Congress' bill establishing Sequoia National Park in 1890 and Yosemite National Park in the same year was undoubtedly influenced by a public letter-writing campaign to preserve the areas, due in part to Muir's popular articles about the giant sequoias and other features of the Sierra.[30] The parks had other backers, including executives of the Southern Pacific Railroad who recognized their value to the growing tourist trade, and farmers in California's expanding agriculture sector in the San Joaquin Valley who recognized the need to protect the Sierra Nevada watershed.

MUIR FINDS YOSEMITE

In the south-central region of the Sierra Nevada lies the lush Yosemite Valley, running over 11km (7 miles) long and 1.5km (nearly a mile) wide, pinioned by 900-metre (2,900-foot) granite cliffs, and thick-grown with white fir, ponderosa pine and California black oak alongside the Merced River. When John Muir first saw it, you can almost hear his breathlessness as he writes:

'*The great Tissiack, or Half-Dome, rising at the upper end of the valley to a height of nearly a mile, is nobly proportioned and life-like,*

the most impressive of all the rocks, holding the eye in devout admiration, calling it back again and again from falls or meadows, or even the mountains beyond – marvelous cliffs, marvelous in sheer dizzy depth and sculpture...Thousands of years have they stood in the sky exposed to rain, snow, frost, earthquake and avalanche, yet they still wear the bloom of youth.'[31]

After his first visit to the Yosemite Valley in 1868, Muir returned the next year to work nearby as a ranch hand, then as a shepherd's hand, and then at a sawmill, eventually recording his thoughts and observations in My First Summer in the Sierra. For several years, the Sierra was his playground and he thought nothing of exploring solo for months at a time, climbing mountains and cliffs with no ropes or equipment, collecting plant samples, sketching and even exploring the interior of glaciers.

The name 'Yosemite' was bestowed upon the valley by early European visitors who heard the local Miwok peoples speaking of a rival tribe, whose name meant 'those who kill'. A more accurate name would be what the Yosemite people called the deep-carved valley they lived in: Awooni, meaning 'large or gaping mouth.' Muir wasn't the first admirer or protector of the Yosemite region. In 1864 Abraham Lincoln and Congress placed a portion of the present-day Yosemite National Park and the Mariposa Grove of giant sequoias under California state protection.

MUIR AND THE CONSERVATIONIST PRESIDENT

In an age when photographic equipment was heavy and cumbersome, Muir made it his mission to reproduce the wild beauty of the Sierra for those in the east who had never seen a mountain range. As a jobbing essayist from the 1870s on, Muir's passionate and voluminously detailed articles may lack the narrative thrust we've come to expect from what we now might call adventure-writing, but were published in some of the most popular newspapers and magazines of the time, including The New York Tribune, Atlantic Monthly and The Century. As Muir published more and more and his public status grew, his influence on public land acquisition culminated with a 1903 camping trip with US President Theodore Roosevelt.

The 65-year-old Muir and Roosevelt, then two years into his first term, visited Mariposa Grove, as well as Sentinel Dome, Glacier Point and the Yosemite Valley. The trip probably inspired the President to incorporate Mariposa Grove into Yosemite National Park. By the end of his second term in 1909, Roosevelt had created five national parks, 18 national monuments, over 50 bird sanctuaries and wildlife refuges, and 150 national forests. Though not an environmentalist in the narrow sense – he was a big game hunter who once boasted of killing over 500 animals on a single safari in Africa, including 29 zebras, 17 lions and 8 hippos – Theodore Roosevelt's passion for preserving large unbroken wild spaces happily aligned with Muir's, even if their reasons for wanting them may have differed. It could be argued that without Muir's counsel, Roosevelt's public land spree might have been far less extensive.

'NO DULL EMPTY HOURS': MUIR'S TRANSFORMATION

Something happened to Muir in the Sierra Nevada – something transformative and lasting. The ragged wanderer surviving on stale bread and thin tea, the amateur botanist-geologist, the university dropout drifting between menial, low-paying jobs, found in the Sierra something far more precious than the goldfields that had inspired such rapacity less than two decades before his arrival. He found his life's work here and conveyed a reason for society to care about the wild places whose vulnerability was not yet widely understood or appreciated.

In Muir's time, US mountain regions were under threat from mining, unchecked livestock grazing and hydroelectric megaprojects. He saw the Sierra and the Cascades and the other ranges he explored as sanctuaries of wildness, a term favoured by essayist Henry David Thoreau, whom Muir had read carefully, and who wrote 'in wildness is the preservation of the world.' If Muir's writings could coalesce into two words, they might be: Mountains Save. If we take his example, seeking out mountain regions can provide lifelong fuel for our quest for meaning and purpose. And preserving these places will also save us from a life crammed into endless grids of industrial development.

Muir's early regard for the Sierra bursts forth out of this journal entry in *My First Summer in the Sierra*, where he is describing sketching on the North Dome, one of the many huge granite walls that frame the Yosemite Valley:

'I would fain draw everything in sight – rock, tree, and leaf. But little can I do beyond mere outlines – marks with meanings like words, readable only to myself – yet I sharpen my pencils and work on as if others might possibly be benefited. Whether these picture-sheets are to vanish like fallen leaves or go to friends like letters, matters not much; for little can they tell to those who have not themselves seen similar wildness, and like a language have learned it. No pain here, no dull empty hours, no fear of the past, no fear of the future. These blessed mountains are so compactly filled with God's beauty, no petty personal hope or experience has room to be.'

While climbing in the Alps in the 1970s, American nature photographer Galen Rowell asked mountaineer Reinhold Messner why Europe's highest range is peppered with hotels, tunnels, cable-cars, railways and towns, while in the western US, whole systems remain relatively untouched. Messner answered, 'You had Muir.'

ODE TO MUIR

We can gauge the present-day measure of John Muir's legacy in a film from Teton Gravity Research, an action sports media company founded in 1996 and head-quartered in Jackson Hole, Wyoming, in the Teton Range of the Rocky Mountains. Its 2018 documentary *Ode to Muir* follows three snowboarders deep into the heart of the John Muir Wilderness in winter, a 650,000-acre slice of high Sierra Nevada consisting of two adjoining National Forest reserves.[32] The narrative consists of John Muir quotes interspersed with banter between the snowboarders. They are led by Jeremy Jones, one of the most skilled big mountain free-riders anywhere, and also the founder of nonprofit Protect Our Winters (POW), an organization dedicated to raising awareness of climate change and how it is impacting snow sports.

Throughout the film, titles draw attention to various conservation milestones, including the 1872 establishment of Yellowstone, the world's first

national park. After Yellowstone, a spate of park and
national monument creation followed for the next
several decades, including in many mountain regions.
In 1964, The Wilderness Act, which protects just over
9 million acres of public land (including the John Muir
Wilderness), passed Congress by a vote of 447 to 13 –
a margin unthinkable in today's polarized legislative
climate in the US. (The text of the Act, penned in large
part by conservationist Howard Zahniser, is a work
of literature in itself, defining the wilderness as 'an
area where the earth and its community of life are
untrammeled by man, where man himself is a visitor
who does not remain.'[33])

The film intersperses these tidbits of US conservation
history with footage of the snowboarders carving big
wind-scoured Sierra bowls, hiking up ridge lines and
camping near icy creeks, with no others in sight. As the
snowboarders approach the Lyell and Maclure glaciers,
we learn that they've lost about 80 per cent of their surface
area since Muir first studied them in the 1870s.

As he and his companions boot-pack up Red Slate
Mountain, Jeremy Jones marvels at this snowbound
happiness-delivery system and what untapped pleasures
it harbours: 'Happiness for me is so easy to achieve and
it doesn't cost a lot of money. How lucky I am for that...
I've spent basically my whole life in the Sierra and
I continue to see huge chunks of terrain for the first
time.' As the athletes descend into old-growth montane
forest, Jones' narrative takes on a more sombre tone.
'You've gotta fall in love with nature, if you want to
protect nature. I don't think our elected officials value
that as much as they used to...The perspectives gained
from being out there – it's everything. [Nature] is one
of our greatest resources and the reality is, if nature fails,
humanity fails.'

The Muir quotes featured in the film dovetail with the
ethos of extreme sports today, for example from The
Mountains of California:

'Few places in this world are more dangerous than home. Fear not, therefore, to try the mountain-passes. They will kill care, save you from deadly apathy, set you free, and call forth every faculty into vigorous, enthusiastic action. Even the sick should try these so-called dangerous passes, because for every unfortunate they kill, they cure a thousand.'

And another from My First Summer in the Sierra:

'June 13. Another glorious Sierra day in which one seems to be dissolved and absorbed and sent pulsing onward we know not where. Life seems neither long nor short, and we take no more heed to save time or make haste than do the trees and stars. This is true freedom, a good practical sort of immortality.'

THE 'FLAWLESS STRENGTH' OF YOSEMITE GRANITE

Muir's beloved Yosemite Valley, and in particular its big granite buttresses, have become a climbers' global convergence point since the 1950s. In 2015, world media descended on the 914-metre (3,000-foot) El Capitan monolith at the valley's western end, as Tommy Caldwell and Kevin Jorgeson completed the first free-climb of the Dawn Wall on the southeast face. (In free-climbing, climbers use a safety rope to stop falls but not to aid their ascent.) Two years later, Alex Honnold free-soloed – climbed with no equipment and no rope to stop a fall – a route up El Cap's southwest face. Muir described El Cap in his book The Yosemite as 'a plain, severely simple, glacier-sculptured face of granite, the end of one of the most compact and enduring of the mountain ridges, unrivaled in height and breadth and flawless strength.'

This successful and first-ever free-solo of the difficult route, which Honnold completed in just four hours, brought rock climbing into the media spotlight to an even greater degree than the Dawn Wall free-climb, with The New York Times proclaiming it 'should be celebrated as one of the greatest athletic feats of any kind ever'. Free-soloing is the purest form of climbing and undoubtedly closest to John Muir in spirit – though it should be added that Muir free-soloed only because he didn't know any other way to climb. Honnold's free-solo is, in contrast, a deliberate return to the simplest (and most dangerous) form of climbing. Muir climbed with no equipment largely because no equipment was available, apart from hemp rope, and also because ultra-minimalist trekking was his ethos. He is credited with several first ascents, all ropeless, including Cathedral Peak, Mount Ritter and Mount Whitney in the Sierra Nevada, and elsewhere in the Pacific Northwest. Fittingly there is a route on the southwest face of El Cap called Muir Wall, named and first ascended in 1965 by T M Herbert and Yvon Chouinard (founder of the outdoor clothing company Patagonia).

It is heartening to know that every young climber today who seeks out the granite of the Sierra will most likely come away knowing something of Muir's legacy. And Muir would probably approve of all the mainstream media attention trained on Yosemite National Park, for he understood that enlarging the role of the Park Service in the eyes of the public will only help protect it from inimical governments or anyone else who would ever seek to weaken the institution.

Shambhala Found

In Tibetan Buddhist writings and oral tradition, Shambhala is a legendary kingdom in a mountain valley in some unspecified but northerly area of the Himalayas, considered an enlightened place whose inhabitants live free from fear, want and disease. (The legend inspired British novelist James Hilton's Shangri-La, the paradise described in his 1933 novel Lost Horizon.) One must undertake a perilous journey though mountains to go there, and success is by no means assured. Into the legend is built a prophecy: that the king of Shambhala will rise up to vanquish evil and usher in a golden age. We can be almost certain that John Muir was unacquainted with Tibetan Buddhism, but in his exploration of the Sierra Nevada and especially in his beloved Yosemite Valley, he found a Shambhala of sorts – an uncorrupted mountain sanctuary. And thanks to his efforts it is not a place apart, but a place open to everyone.

Bhutan and the Mountain Way of Life

Straddling the eastern ridges of the Himalayas, Bhutan is defined by mountains. Apart from the slender Duars Plain in the south near the Indian border, all of this small, landlocked country is either glaciated peaks, swooping valleys, alpine meadows or montane forest. Roughly 72 per cent of the country is forested and, as mandated in its constitution, the country will always preserve 60 per cent of its land under forest cover.

A former monarchy that became a parliamentary democracy in 2008, Bhutan maintains a Gross National Happiness (GNH) Index. Bhutanese King Jigme Singye Wangchuck coined the term 'Gross National Happiness' in 1972, believing it to be more important than Gross Domestic Product. Apart from exhaustive reports on happiness, GNH provides a foundation for its government and citizenry to encourage sustainable development over unchecked economic progress, and to highlight the many facets of wellbeing.

Mountains hold a central and sacred place here. Unlike any other country on earth, this Buddhist kingdom forbids mountaineering on peaks above 6,000 metres (19,700 feet). This includes what is considered to be the world's highest unclimbed mountain, Gangkhar Puensum at 7,570 metres (24,800 feet). With countless Buddhist deities believed to reside in the mountains, the government in the 1990s decided to close them to climbers. This decision might also in part be due to the glaring environmental impacts of overcrowding on Mount Everest.

Bhutan's Gross National Happiness

These are a few of the results from Bhutan's most recent Gross National Happiness Report:

- 89 per cent of the population report 'normal mental wellbeing'
- 82 per cent of Bhutanese feel 'highly responsible' for conserving their natural environment
- 90 per cent rated their health as 'good', 'very good' or 'excellent'
- 64 per cent describe their sense of belonging to their local community as 'very strong'; a further 32 per cent describe it as 'somewhat strong'.[34]

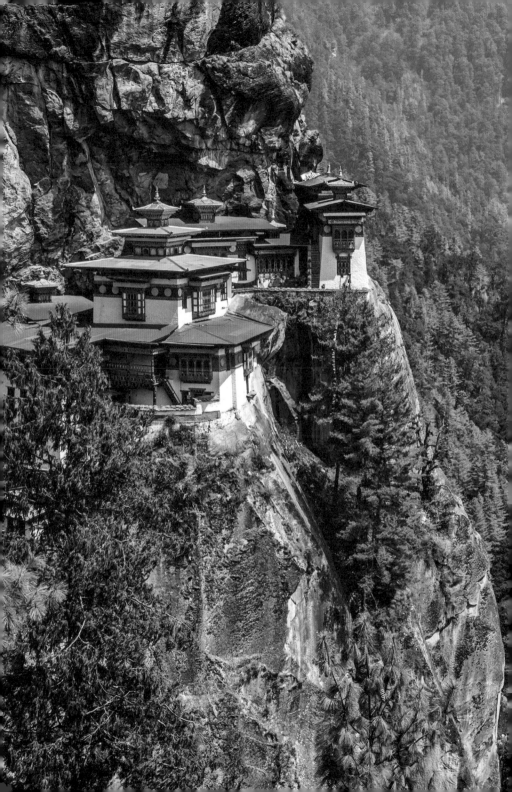

Ski-Mountaineering and Self-Knowledge

Based in Revelstoke, British Columbia, ski-mountaineer Greg Hill has completed many first descents but is best known for climbing and skiing 2 million vertical feet (609km/378 miles) in 2010. This feat required him to ascend (and then descend) 71 mountains in North and South America in one calendar year – and he did about half of them solo. The following year, *Men's Fitness* magazine not surprisingly named Hill one of the 'Top 25 Fittest Guys in the World'. He has summited and skied over 220 mountains all over the globe, including in Scandinavia, the Alps, Nepal and Pakistan.

For Hill, the mountains represent a bottomless source of energy and happiness. When I spoke to him he pointed out a history of depression among the men in his family but said he has avoided that illness. 'In my family there are some "dark passengers" but I don't feel I have that, and maybe it's because I've spent so much time working on myself in the mountains. The mountains have given me time to work on getting rid of all the clutter that makes you focus on things that don't matter. I believe being out there helps you figure out how to be happy. I started ski-mountaineering because it just made sense to me. At every level I was at, I'd say, "Now what's next? I just toured 5,000 feet – I wonder if I can tour 6,000? I wonder if I can tour 10,000?" I remember my second year of ski-mountaineering and my partners were always tired at the end of the day and I was thinking "I have so much more energy...what else can I be doing?"'

PEELING BACK THE LAYERS

Hill is the first North American to climb and ski Mont Blanc in a day (11 hours) and has pioneered many British Columbian traverses, including the Monashee Range (in southeastern British Columbia, stretching into Washington State) over a period of three weeks, at an incredible one-peak-per-day pace. In the midst of his sky-touching heroics, sustained by off-the-charts endurance, Hill is still able to make unexpected discoveries about himself. 'To know my limits is to know who I am,' he said. 'When I'm into a 20-hour day I can start to peel back my layers of worry: you peel back this layer and that layer and eventually you're so tired that you don't care if people like you, and you don't care what you're wearing…The idea is to figure out how to peel all those layers back right to your core person and make sure he's happy and centred. And then the layers can go back on and they won't matter as much because the core is good.

'A lot of our issues come from the clutter we're taught to lay on, every day. And we have to just muddle our way through it. And that makes us unhappy because we haven't got that inner core of happiness to help us deal with all the outer layers. If you take away someone's phone and take them out to where nothing matters but where they are, and what's happening around them, it simplifies everything. It gives people that time to just stop and think.'

SELF-RELIANCE

I asked Hill how he manages risk when ski-mountaineering. 'Often I'm out touring with people and I see that they aren't observant of all the hazards around us. There's always about 20 per cent of my brain that's focused on the hazards and evaluating them constantly.

And because I know that 20 per cent is focusing on that, I can free up the other 80 per cent to enjoy and to understand how lucky I am to be there.' To illustrate how crucial it is to be always managing risk, Hill described ski-mountaineering a peak in Nepal with a less-than-cohesive group. 'They were all about ego and conquering the peak and I was about working with the mountain. I was the only guy with a shovel and a beacon… but I learned something, because I saw how important it is to have partners with the same risk tolerance and the same thought-patterns.

'The confidence that comes with self-reliance is key: once you develop the skills and you know your team is strong, you can…*almost* do whatever you want. The rules of the mountains make a lot of sense to me. They're natural, not man-made, concocted rules. And obviously I love to watch the sun glint off the snow or the wind blow through the trees – I don't consider myself a spiritual person but mountains bring me peace and raw beauty. In my successes, my failures and all my challenges, I've developed an inner confidence that eventually echoes into everything else I do. I want to try to teach that to my kids, give them that confidence.'

~~~~~~~~~~~~~~~~~

Protecting Our Winters

In the last few years, Greg Hill (see page 87) has turned his focus towards sustainability in the mountains. In an effort to reduce his carbon footprint, he sold his truck and snowmobile and bought an electric car; he has now climbed or skied over 60 mountains self-powered, without the use of fossil fuels. He also joined Protect Our Winters (POW) as an Ambassador, and now he travels widely for speaking engagements and co-presents with other athletes.

I asked Hill if, as a mountain athlete, he is more aware of climate change. 'It's more obvious to us in the mountains,' he said. 'I've been skiing Rogers Pass since 1999. The Illecillewaet Glacier has shrunk back hundreds of feet. It is the longest-studied glacier in North America. When Mary Vaux was studying the glacier [the American naturalist photographed and wrote about glaciers throughout the Rockies, and first visited Illecillewaet in 1887], it was 900 metres (2,950 feet) lower than it is today. And in Revelstoke there's a glacial tongue on Mount Begbie. To me it looks like the front legs of a polar bear. And I'm just waiting for those front legs to fall off.'

~~~~~~~~~~~~~~~~~

The Gift of Mountains

American outdoor gear and apparel manufacturer Patagonia is an exemplar of the sustainability movement in business. Its founder, anti-businessman and former pro rock-climber Yvon Chouinard, once wrote: 'It's business that has to take the majority of the blame for being the enemy of nature.' Founded in 1973 and headquartered in Ventura, California, Patagonia revels in its own paradoxes – the company famously placed an ad in The New York Times advising consumers, 'Don't Buy This Shirt', advocating a buy-less approach and underlining its free repair and recycling service for everything it makes. Named for the remote mountain region shared by Chile and Argentina where Chouinard used to climb – a name, an early product catalogue explained, evocative of 'romantic visions of glaciers tumbling into fjords, jagged windswept peaks, gauchos and condors' – Patagonia frequently advocates for public land and environmental protections. The only television advertisement the company has ever released was not about its products but about threats to US national parks and monuments.

Patagonia chooses just a handful of mountain athletes as its brand ambassadors – informal public relations representatives who not only wear Patagonia duds but live and breathe the ethos and bring their own angle to it. One of these ambassadors is Quebec-born, British Columbia-based pro snowboarder Marie-France Roy. Roy, or MFR as she is known, won early acclaim as an X Games competitor before transitioning into filming backcountry snowboarding segments. Frequently topping reader polls for Athlete of the Year and Video Part of the Year in industry publications, today she lives in an ultra-sustainable cob home that she built on Vancouver Island.

'MY WHOLE PATH CHANGED'

I asked MFR to describe the role of mountains in her life. 'When my parents separated when I was nine, my mother left, and the mountains saved us,' she said. Her father raised MFR and her two older brothers and needed a way to keep everybody, including himself, active. 'My Dad said, "If we're going to pick a sport, I want it to be one I can do, too. So if the three of you help me clean the house, and stack wood, I will get you season passes every year [at Le Massif de Charlevoix ski resort, northeast of Quebec City] as long as you get summer jobs to help pay for your gear." And so of course we were stoked and that was the start for me, going to Le Massif every weekend, trying to keep up with my brothers and their friends...I don't know where I'd be today if it wasn't for that.

'As a kid it gave me so much because I was very shy and snowboarding gave me something – all of a sudden I was good at something. I was so intimidated by my brothers' friends but it pushed me to become comfortable in uncomfortable situations. And it made me want to travel to other mountains. I never intended to become a snowboarder for a living. Initially I studied Ecology but I decided to take a year in Whistler to experience the mountains before I got a real job. That's when my whole path changed. I entered a few events, it went really well, I got sponsored, I got to travel, and since then my life has really been in the mountains. High up in the alpine, the closest to the top of the atmosphere, this is where the snow melts into the rivers, and then the rivers become our water source. It all starts here.'

OLYMPIC TRAVERSE

I asked MFR to take us inside a big-mountain wilderness snowboarding trip. 'We traversed Olympic National Park around Mount Olympus (pictured opposite) [in northwest Washington State] for eight days in spring 2018 for Patagonia,' she said. 'It's not a common route, it's way out there and we had to explain to the rangers where we were going and they were like, "No one goes there, there are no trails!". They didn't want to give us the permit. One of my friends had snowboarded on Denali and the other had done a lot of glacier camping and he said, "We've studied this!" And so they let us go. It was one of the most fabulous experiences

of my life but it was really hard: halfway through our mission we almost turned around due to weather, and we only had a certain amount of food and if we kept going we might run out. Some of the glacier terrain was a big question mark, most of the route was bushwhacking, we got lost a few times, we splitboarded all the way up this glacier only to realize that we didn't have to...once we looked over the edge it was sheer cliffs. But I love not knowing what's behind the edge. As much as it can be stressful and scary – a few times I was a bit scared – I just love the whole aspect and the mix of emotions.'

How does MFR handle uncertainty and risk in a wilderness such as Olympic National Park – knowing she is beyond rescue if anything goes wrong? 'If you're not scared sometimes in the mountains, that's a bad thing,' she said. 'I try not to be too greedy about what I get out of the mountains. When we were halfway through the [Olympic] trip, looking out over the peaks we were about to go into, we sat there staring at them and they were all socked in [with snow]. And we all agreed, maybe it's OK to turn around. It's good not to be greedy! But we went on anyway...You can't have too much ego about it. We get so much from the mountains. We extract our pleasure from them and also our resources, but we don't always treat them with appropriate respect and exchange, I find. And you can't always come into the mountains and get what you want, on a snowboard trip or whatever. And that's OK. The mountains are boss.'

THE FLOW STATE

I asked MFR what I always want to ask extreme mountain athletes: to describe the thought patterns that accompany skiing or boarding in dangerous places, where a fall could easily result in death. 'I'm flying downhill with gravity and it's an incredible feeling; you want to go as fast as you can without falling and that's the game. It's a bit like meditation where you try to breathe and free your mind up. When you find yourself on a challenging line, your body, your brain knows that everything else has to move out so you can focus on this one task. This state of focus, once you start dropping in, is weird – there's no room for anything else. There's lots of fear before I'm dropping into a line but once I do, I'm not scared any more. I'm focused and I'm flowing.

'When you're in that flow state, you feel invincible. It doesn't last forever, and you might make mistakes once in a while, but it's incredible what you can achieve once you find yourself in that state, when you are in tune with your body and your senses and your surroundings. And you have to be in tune with the mountain: it's survival. You have to be aware of sounds, movement, landmarks and what's at the bottom. And once you get to the bottom and you've nailed it, there's not a better feeling. And when you're self-powered, I love it even more. When you're splitboarding and hike it up there, it's more fulfilling. You can say, "I put a lot of work into this, I had doubts, but I studied the snow, I listened to my instincts." When it's your third time trying this line and you finally nail it and you did it with your own power? The mountain let you have this feeling. You were meant to be here: it was her gift.'

What is Flow?

Psychologists define a flow state as being totally in tune with the activity you are performing, being highly focused and working toward a set of clear goals. It could also be described as being 'in the zone'. This can occur in many different types of activities, including sports, playing an instrument, painting, writing or playing a game such as chess. Being in a flow state leads to better performance, and can also result in improved skill development and learning, as well as greater enjoyment of the activity, a feeling of serenity and a feeling of achievement – all things that benefit us psychologically.

Flow states only occur, however, when the activity offers just the right level of challenge. If it's too easy, you have to increase the challenge to achieve a flow state; if it's too difficult, you have to learn new skills to reduce the challenge.

Mountains and Human Interaction

A further dimension of spending time in the high mountains relates to human interaction. Marie-France Roy explained: 'It's a great way to meet people and connect with people in a really healthy environment. Meeting in the mountains is probably the best Tinder there is…you can't get away with as much in the mountains. If you're not respectful or behaving a certain way, you might not get invited again. There are consequences; you have to behave. And learn from each other. At first you have to go with people who are better than you. And that starts a cycle of learning and teaching.'

ENVIRONMENTAL FOOTPRINT RECKONING

MFR traces the evolution of her environmental awareness from her early memories to her pro riding days. 'My time in the mountains is a reconfirmation of everything I've thought as a kid. My first connection with the issue came at a very early age: I don't know how or why but I feel it was playing outside so much and being curious about everything around me, all the habitats. I could tell that humans had a direct impact on nature in an unsustainable way. I could tell – even before I knew the word "pollution" – what pollution was. That was always a subconscious worry I had growing up. That's why I went to school for ecology: I wanted to be a part of protecting it. We all know the story about the Blackcomb Glacier receding [also known as the Horstman Glacier, on Blackcomb Mountain, British Columbia]. That's a strong visual, it hits you. And also the forest fires [2018 was the worst fire season on record there]. It's scary to me that climate change isn't an emergency in everybody's mind. It is shocking to me.'

MFR doesn't shy away from holding herself to account. 'With all my travelling and sponsorships, I started feeling a lot of guilt. I was pursuing my own selfish goals. I was using snowmobiles, I was cat-boarding and heli-boarding, it's part of the job. I was promoting consumption of product. And I didn't feel I could speak about the environment when I had such a big footprint. I even thought about quitting snowboarding and living in the woods. And then I wondered, "Is that really the best thing I can do as an individual, to make a difference?" And it took me a while to realize that it would be stupid to give up something I've worked so hard towards. And maybe my influence could be greater if I can use my connections, all I've seen on my travels, and my influence with brands, to make a difference.

'And yes my footprint is still an issue, but at the same

time, we all have a footprint. Climate change and the environmental destruction we're seeing now is too big of an issue to be fixed overnight by a small group of people, and if we're waiting for people who have no footprint at all to resolve it, we're doomed. We're all victims of this fossil fuel economy we've created. Even though I have a considerable footprint, the reason I speak up is to change that, so we can all continue to do the things we love.'

Recently she joined Protect Our Winters (POW) as an Ambassador. I asked MFR if she's an athlete first, or an activist first; she said the question wasn't exactly relevant. 'I don't know what to call myself,' she said. 'I'm just a human being who's trying to do what I love and trying to speak out for what I love. These terms sometimes cause confusion. I like the word "environmental" but so many people are afraid of that word. It's like "feminist". We all need the environment so we're all environmentalists in a way.'

The View from Mauna Loa: Mountains and Climate Change

The words 'climate change' can summon a cascade of bristly political associations which threaten to overwhelm our understanding of the slow-motion planetary crisis they denote. Utter the words at a dinner party and the chances are fair you will cast a pall over the evening as thick and choking as a coal-fired power-plant smokestack.

The words may cause politicized discomfort but growing choruses of scientists are offering more proofs of climate change: largely due to carbon emissions and deforestation, by warming the atmosphere and the oceans, humans are hastening it at an unprecedented rate.

Since 1958, a weather station and observatory has stood on a small plateau of hardened lava not far below the summit of earth's largest volcano, Mauna Loa, on the main island of Hawaii. Started up by scientist Charles David Keeling of the Scripps Institution of Oceanography, the Mauna Loa observatory has monitored changes in the atmosphere for 60 years. The NOAA (the US National Oceanic and Atmospheric Administration) began taking measurements here in 1974. Due to the elevation of Mauna Loa (4,169 metres/13,700 feet) and its isolated location in the middle of the Pacific Ocean, researchers consider the air to be ideal for testing, for it is mostly beyond the reach of the adulterating influences of human-caused pollution and local vegetation.

In 2018, researchers from NOAA and Scripps announced a sobering milestone. In April and May, the level of carbon dioxide averaged more than 410 parts per million (ppm), the highest rates ever recorded. 'CO_2 levels have been growing at all-time record rates because consumption of coal, oil and natural gas are also at historically high levels,' said NOAA scientist Pieter Tans in a press release. 'Today's emissions will still be trapping heat in the atmosphere thousands of years from now.'[35]

The growth rate of CO_2 in the atmosphere has been accelerating ever since the Mauna Loa observatory started keeping records. In the 1980s it increased on average by 1.6ppm per year; during the last decade, that average increased to 2.2ppm.

'Many of us had hoped to see the rise of CO_2 slowing by now, but sadly that isn't the case,' said Charles David Keeling's son, scientist Ralph Keeling, who now oversees the Mauna Loa observatory for Scripps. But Keeling added a more optimistic note: 'It could still happen in the next decade or so if renewables replace enough fossil fuels.'[36]

VANISHING LABORATORIES

Glaciated mountain environments in particular are the open-air laboratories where more proofs of climate change are unfolding, or more precisely melting, before our eyes. Today, earth is in an interglacial period (the Holocene) without continent-wide ice sheets – and though 'inter' suggests glaciers will return some day, many of those remaining are in rapid retreat. While prehistoric glacial subsidence was a slow-motion, multi-millennial process, scientists today are documenting startling rates of glacial shift and collapse.

At present, about 10 per cent of land area on Earth is covered with glacial ice, or roughly 15 million square kilometres (5,800,000 square miles), locked into high alpine and polar regions. Glaciers store an estimated 75 per cent of Earth's fresh water. A University of Colorado study used satellite data to demonstrate that mountain glaciers shed up to 571 trillion pounds (259 trillion kilograms) of ice per year, adding about 30 per cent to the total recorded global sea level rise during the study period.[37] Clearly, mountains play a large and under-appreciated role holding Earth in balance.

MELTDOWN AT THE CAMP OF CHAMPIONS

It is occasionally the case that a single public event or utterance comes to symbolize the moment when a crisis spills out past the purview of scientists or others with specialized knowledge. For the impact of climate change in mountains, one could argue that moment came in 2017 on a shrinking glacier on Blackcomb Mountain, British Columbia. Snowboarder and entrepreneur Ken Achenbach founded the Camp of Champions in 1989 at the Horstman Glacier on Blackcomb, where over

the next 27 years it hosted countless young snowboarders
and skiers in the summer months, connecting them with
coaches, many of them former Olympians.

In an extraordinary open letter posted on Facebook
and addressed to campers and parents, Achenbach
announced the camp had to close: climate change had
decimated the glacier. 'To give you an idea of how much
melting has happened the last few years, in 2015 alone the
glacier lost 35 vertical feet of ice,' wrote Achenbach.
'Campers now load on the T-Bar 3 towers up the glacier
from where we loaded in 1989. The rock I used to sit on to
do up my bindings in 1989 is 140 or more feet up the cliff
wall above the camp park...Simply put, it's the effects of
global warming. I wanted to give you an exceptional
experience, and now I can't. After 28 years my dream is
over...I refuse to let you fly and drive from all over the
world to ride a park that wouldn't even be worth driving
from Vancouver for...As painful as it will be for everyone
involved and as life shattering as it will be for me, I have to
take the only honourable option that is open to me, even
if it means the end of The Camp of Champions and my
reputation.' In 2017 the Camp of Champions declared
bankruptcy. It is tough to imagine a more immediate
account of the impact of climate change on snow sports
in the mountains.

Josh Hydeman, Glacier Explorer

A different sort of mountain professional finds beauty in rapidly melting glaciers. With photographs published widely, including in *National Geographic* and *Outside*, Oregon-based photographer-explorer Josh Hydeman has captured the seldom-seen, mutable world of glacial caves – water-carved hollows and tunnels in the guts of these giant, rock-flecked bulldozers of ice (examples opposite and on page 107).

Sandy Glacier, on the western side of Mount Hood in Oregon's Cascade Range, is a remnant of an ice cap that covered the massif during the Pleistocene era, a mass of fossil ice containing air bubbles and organic material crucial to the study of life and atmospheric conditions over thousands of years. In 2012, explorers Brent McGregor and Eddy Cartaya mapped the Sandy cave system to a length of over 2 km (1¼ miles). Three years later, Josh Hydeman explored the system with a team of scientists led by Andreas Pflitsch of Ruhr University in Germany, who studies the impact of climate change in glacial caves. During the Pflitsch expedition, the navigable passages ran less than 300 metres (980 feet). According to Hydeman, today the cave is much reduced and no longer worth visiting.

THE HAZARDS OF GLACIER CAVES

I asked Hydeman how challenging it was to shoot inside the Sandy Glacier. 'There's a lot of rock- and icefall,' he said. 'Once, a car-sized chunk of ice slid off the wall about six metres away; I was just turning on my DSLR and focusing and we could hear the ice cracking as I pressed record. And exiting Pure Imagination [a now-collapsed cave] there's a debris chute above the mouth with so many rocks coming down, you need a spotter to tell you that *now* would be the time to run as fast as you can. In summer, morning is the safest time to go into a cave, since the sun hasn't affected the ice yet. But around sunset, the water is raging – a small river flowing throughout the cave – so much white noise you have to yell to communicate. In winter it's much quieter, more echoey. You're always surprised by the changing features: how alive these caves are. They really have personalities. The level of difficulty is condition- and season-specific, and it might take rope work and crampons to see the entire cave. In winter, there's a very icy, sideways traverse on angles anywhere from 25 to 40 degrees. In summer, it's almost as challenging because it's very steep talus with lots of moving rock.

'There have been times when conditions made it easy to visit the cave, and a lot of photographers did, but they'd just go in, take a couple of shots, and leave,' Hydeman continued. 'If you spend a week there in the summer, however, the amount of time you're inside adds to the danger – just like a mountain climber doing a ridge traverse. Once I was shooting a sunset rainbow in a small waterfall pouring out of a moulin [a vertical shaft in a glacier formed by water percolating down from the top] and a piece of rock the size of a lawn chair came down through it...But it's not like we're scared the whole time. You look at the ceiling and pay attention to where rocks are and you just move quickly. And you need to go with the right people. For the 2015 expedition, we had walkie-talkie communication with Search and Rescue; that kind of psychological support lets you get a lot of caving done.'

THE PACE OF CHANGE

As a photographer, Hydeman has witnessed change in the Sandy Glacier caves more vividly than anyone. 'This place is so strikingly beautiful that my memory of it is very detailed. So when I revisited it was easy to see the differences; many features I photographed were no longer there.'

I asked what first attracted him to glacier caves. 'First it was beauty,' he said. 'Then I attended the International Workshop on Ice Caves where I learned that there's a sense of urgency about them among scientists. They want to collect samples from ice caves before they melt. Spending

so much time photographing these places has been an ongoing learning process. Being able to freeze these moments with photography makes sense to me. I can help leave a record.' As part of an ongoing study of climate change and mountain glaciers, Andreas Pflitsch's team installed data loggers in Sandy and other Pacific Northwest glacier caves, including one on the summit of Mount Rainier.

A MOUNTAINEER IN REVERSE

Hydeman relies on rock caves for the bulk of his photography. In his work in some of the world's deepest caves, he is a new-breed mountain explorer – he explores their intestines. He is a mountaineer in reverse.

In the Seven Devils Mountains of Idaho lies Papoose Cave – the deepest in the state and probably one of the top ten deepest in the US (though as cavers continue to explore, the list is constantly revising). Here and in a nearby, smaller cave known as Ta'c Wees, Hydeman has shot and explored extensively. In June 2018, snowmelt was raging through many of the limestone passages when Hydeman and a team of cavers entered Papoose. With a long drive to the end of a logging road (the Seven Devils range and lowlands lie within the Nez Perce-Clearwater National Forest, thick with fir, spruce and pine) and then a steep hike just to reach the entrances, Papoose and Ta'c Wees are not much frequented by anyone other than deadly serious cavers. They're even less frequented when they're filled with frigid whitewater. 'These caves are on the side of a mountain and they're challenging, they're cold,' said Hydeman. 'Ta'c Wees hasn't seen a ton of exploration.' Even dressed in cave suits overtop thick wetsuits, it was so cold in the caves that if Hydeman ever found himself at a standstill even for a moment, he did push-ups or squats to produce body warmth. 'There was tons of water and it was 37°F (2.7°C) which is pretty cold when you're completely soaked,' he added.

In Papoose, Hydeman and caver Jeff Wurst chose to climb up a waterfall – there was another way around it but they wanted the experience and Hydeman wanted the photo. 'That was really exciting,' he said. 'Climbing that rope, you're just getting so pummelled on the head that at points you couldn't breathe for 30 seconds and then you'd have to try to push yourself out of the stream of water for a breath of air and then continue to climb.' Hydeman ascended ahead of Wurst to position himself to take the shot. 'I had some climbing ascenders attached to the rope that he's on because that water was so forceful it could knock you over…I had to fight not to fall over in that waterfall because I was in a precarious place trying to photograph. So I was holding a camera in one hand, a flash in the other and then I had this tether from my harness with a climbing ascender on the rope so that I wouldn't just tumble over. The current pushes you pretty hard, you would need to forcefully weight yourself, physically push against the flow of the water just to be able to stand up.'

I asked Hydeman what he takes away from these expeditions to places visited by so few others. 'There is a renewing quality that I get from going into these spaces that is really exciting to me and I feel I can share that with these images.'

CHAPTER 5

ENHANCING THE BENEFITS
OF THE MOUNTAINS

~~~~~~~~~~

"Then, to the music
of golden ankle bells,
the noble ones will lift
you on their shoulders in
a sedan chair of the gods
and carry you like a load
of cotton over the wall
of snow mountains."

— Rinpungpa

The mountain environment can offer us a range of health benefits, both physical and emotional. Whether you are visiting for a day, a week, or you are lucky enough to live in the mountains, it's important to make the most of your time there to reap the maximum rewards.

Immersion in a natural environment is beneficial, whatever you are doing there, even if it's as simple as enjoying a picnic overlooking an inspiring view. However, there are many other activities on offer and this chapter suggests a few of them. However you spend your time in the mountains, remember to switch off your phone and only use it to make emergency calls or as a trail-finding tool. If at all possible, leave it at home to give yourself a break from technology.

Creative Pursuits

Being in a mountain environment can encourage creativity (*see* page 47). We know from research that creating something boosts our wellbeing and we find it very fulfilling, so why not use the mountains to inspire you? Many different activities can harness this creativity.

Painting and Sketching

Mountains have been inspiring artists to reach for their brushes for many centuries, and early adventurers like John Muir recorded the landscapes they visited with pen or pencil.

Painting or drawing a landscape creates a stronger connection with that environment than simply passing through it. It takes time and focus to create even a simple sketch and requires you to sit still and look closely at the view in front of you, the same skills used when practising mindfulness (*see* page 114).

Your level of skill is not important – the process is just as beneficial as the outcome. If you don't usually draw or paint, try a basic sketch with pencil and paper and choose a view or mountain feature that you find particularly appealing.

Photography

Taking the time to look closely enough at the landscape to photograph it will be as beneficial as painting or sketching, and might be more accessible to many. A simple camera or smartphone can produce impressive results, and the process will slow you down and make you really look around you. Close-up detail shots can be just as absorbing as huge mountain vistas, so try a range of different framing techniques.

Creative Writing

If you are happier using words rather than images to create, settle down on a picnic blanket or comfortable rock and take out your notebook and pen. Whether it's poetry or prose, related to the scenery around you or not, the setting should spur creativity. If you can't think of anything else to write, try composing a haiku about the mountains. A haiku is a traditional form of Japanese poetry consisting of three lines. The first and last lines should have five syllables, while the middle line should have seven. The lines don't have to rhyme, but it can still be a challenge to write something that is worthy of your surroundings.

Problem Solving

If you need to think clearly – perhaps to plan something you are working on, or solve a vexing problem – the mountain setting might inspire you to find the solution you need. Take a notebook and pen, sit somewhere with a view and allow your mind to wander a little. Not only should the setting boost your creativity and clear your mind, the distance from home and humanity should offer perspective and allow you to approach the problem in a calm and positive way.

Wellbeing Activities

One of the greatest benefits of a natural setting is the relaxation effects it offers. Research shows that a natural, as opposed to an urban, environment lowers heart rate, lowers blood pressure and reduces the release of hormones such as cortisol, associated with stress.[10] It makes sense to double these relaxation benefits by practising wellbeing activities while in a mountain environment, such as mindfulness, meditation or yoga, which are known to have powerful relaxation benefits in their own right.

MINDFULNESS

Mindfulness is becoming more and more popular as research shows this self-help tool really can work. Mindfulness is about being fully aware of the moment we are in. Most of us spend more time mentally in the past or future than in the present and we miss a lot by not being present in the present. Practising mindfulness is about making a conscious decision to pay attention to the here and now, and do it non-judgementally – that is by dismissing the endless judgements we make about ourselves, about others and about the things around us.

The Benefits of Mindfulness

Many studies have shown that with regular practice, mindfulness can lower blood pressure, heart rate and levels of the hormone cortisol, all associated with stress. It can also boost the immune system and increase energy levels.[38]

Mindfulness has been shown to reduce feelings of anxiety and depression,[39] and can help overcome substance abuse.[40] It can reduce mind wandering and rumination,[41] boost positive emotions and self-esteem and improve quality of life.[42] Another study has shown mindfulness can improve concentration, memory and cognitive function.[43]

Mindfulness Research

Many studies have shown that practicing mindfulness can produce positive effects on psychological wellbeing, reducing stress and anxiety and improving overall happiness. However, one study at the University of Massachusetts Medical School[44] showed that mindfulness can produce physical changes in the brain after only eight weeks. These changes occur in the areas of the brain involved in mind-wandering and the regulation of emotions, learning, memory, the ability to take another perspective, empathy and compassion.

The physical changes in the brains of those who practised mindfulness for eight weeks were accompanied by a reduction in levels of the stress hormone cortisol, and the participants reported that they felt less stressed and less anxious. They also said that they experienced fewer instances of their mind wandering, and reported an increase in their quality of life – and all of this in just eight weeks.

Mindfulness Tips

• Focus on the things around you, really noticing the smallest details.

• When your mind inevitably wanders, just simply bring it back to the present moment, without judgement, as many times as necessary.

• Be kind to yourself and stay calm and focused – it takes some practice so don't get frustrated if your mind wanders a lot to start with.

Use All Five Senses

- VISION – notice the play of light and shade on the landscape as clouds move across the sky. Watch the clouds moving and changing shape. Compare the colours and textures of the different features that make up the view in front of you, the patches of forest, heath, bare rock. Examine the small details around you: the mosses, lichens, tree bark, stones.

- HEARING – noises can sound more distant in the mountains. Can you hear the wind? Listen for the sound of the trees rustling in the breeze, the cries of birds of prey, noises from people far below you. What sound are your feet making on the paths underfoot?

- SCENT – mountain air usually smells clean and fresh. Can you pick out any other smells, such as wildflowers, tree sap or moist earth?

- TOUCH – as you walk, feel the differences between the surfaces you are walking on – hard rock, soft patches of grass and so on. Use your fingers to feel to explore the textures around you – cool, hard rocks, rough or smooth tree bark, soft or spiky grass, snow if it's cold.

- TASTE – take a few deep breaths through your mouth to taste the air. Can you taste anything? Take out any snacks you have and eat them mindfully, really tasting the nuances of the food. Trail mix is a good one to try for this. Take each element separately and really experience its flavour. Then take a small handful of mix and slowly chew, seeing whether you can identify the flavours of the individual elements.

Mindfulness Exercise 1:
Use your senses

Mountains are the essence of permanence and continuity and can make us feel very grounded and part of the bigger picture. Find a patch of bare rock and sit on it, if possible, arranging yourself in a comfortable, relaxed position. If it isn't too cold, take off your shoes and place the soles of your feet on the rock. If not, place the palms of your hands directly on the rock. Aim to spend about 10 minutes on this exercise.

- First look closely at the rock – is it jagged or smooth, what colours can you see in it, are there patches or flecks of different minerals?

- Feel the temperature of the rock against your skin. Does it feel very cold or has it been warmed by the sun?

- Concentrate on the texture. Draw your hand or foot over the surface. Does it feel hard, porous, gravelly, rough or smooth? Are there crystals poking above the surface or has it been weathered smooth?

- Think about the depth of the rock beneath you. Think about the continuity of rock reaching down and down to the earth's crust far below, one continuous massif of rock anchored to the earth.

- See yourself perched on the mountain, a tiny figure on an enormous chunk of rock in a vast landscape.

Mindfulness Exercise 2: Notice your surroundings

This exercise is about looking down at the world from a height. The feeling of detachment from society this gives, from being outside but looking in, helps engender a sense of perspective and can make life's problems seem less significant. Choose a high spot with an extensive view and make yourself comfortable. You can use a pair of binoculars for this exercise if you like.

- First take in the general scene. What can you see? Are there areas of habitation, towns or villages maybe, or individual houses? Are there areas of forest or agriculture, bodies of water such as rivers or lakes?

- Look more closely at the different colours of these different features. What pattern do they make – geometric shapes, a rough patchwork, or uneven sprawling areas? Is there a repeating pattern?

- What can you see moving below you? Depending on the landscape, there might be birds or animals, either wild or domestic. You might see the wind blowing the trees, waterfalls flowing, even human activities such as vehicles moving.

- Can you see any individual people or animals in the landscape? Take the time to look closely. If you spot any, can you gauge their activities?

- Spend 10 minutes really focusing on the scene below you, clearing your mind of all other thoughts as you notice all the details in the landscape.

MEDITATION

The connection between mountains and the Buddhist practice of meditation may not seem immediately apparent but is in fact close, largely due to Tibetan Buddhism and its roots in the Himalayan 'roof of the world'. One could say that Tibetan Buddhism is inseparable from the Himalayan peaks that serve as worshippers' guardian deities, such as Kawakarpo. Tibetan Buddhism's prominence in the West is due in part to the *cause célèbre* popularity of the Dalai Lama, the top monk and Tibet's head of state until the Chinese began their occupation of the kingdom in 1959. The Dalai Lama now lives in exile in northwestern India on the lower slopes of the Himalaya.

Whether Buddhist or not, everyone can benefit from a session of meditation, which will feel all the more powerful if you try it in a mountain setting, allowing you to really connect with the landscape around you.

The Benefits of Meditation

Regular meditation leads to a range of psychological and physiological health benefits.[45]

- Reduces anxiety and stress

- Lowers blood pressure

- Boosts feelings of happiness

- Heightens self-confidence and self-esteem

- Boosts the production of serotonin, the happy hormone

- Reduces overthinking and rumination

- Helps to strengthen the immune system

- Decreases headaches or muscle pain, related to tension

- Increases energy levels

- Enhances creativity

- Improves concentration

A Mountain Meditation

Sit on the ground or on a rock in a stable, comfortable position with your body balanced over your hips, your hands in your lap and your shoulders and arms relaxed and free from tension. Close your eyes and start by paying attention to your breath. Don't try to change it, just observe it as it comes and goes. After a minute or two, open your eyes and look around you.

Gradually become aware of the mountain you are sitting on, sensing its magnificence and sheer volume, its top high in the sky and its base rooted in the earth. Feel the shape of the mountain beneath you, its sloping sides and massive weight. As you continue to focus on your breath, feel you are part of the mountain, an ageless presence unmoving yet alive.

Become aware of the patches of light and shade changing on the surface of the mountain as clouds move across the sun, or the sun moves across the sky. Think of gusts of wind buffeting the surface and showers of rain drenching the rock. Imagine clouds plunging the mountain into obscurity, then clearing to allow the sun to warm the rock. The surface of the mountain is continually changing as the weather changes hour by hour, day by day. Yet the mountain is unwavering through time.

We can feel in ourselves that same core of stillness and strength, unmoving despite all the changes and challenges life throws our way. The essence of us remains the same through all the ups and downs, the turmoil and the tranquility. Recognize that sunshine always returns after a storm and, like the mountain, we can remain unmoved.

YOGA AT ALTITUDE

The practice of yoga has been developed over thousands of years and is more popular than ever today. Many people appreciate its spiritual value but others simply enjoy the serenity and sense of calm it offers, as well as the physical benefits of strength and flexibility.

- **YOGA RETREATS** have been around as long as yoga itself and many take place in isolated mountain settings. More and more are being offered as time-out from busy Western lives, and it can be hugely beneficial to spend several days or a week doing yoga in a mountain setting, cut off from the stresses of daily life.

- **MOUNTAINSIDE PRACTICE** If you have tried yoga before and are familiar with some of the poses, try taking your yoga mat when you visit the mountains. Find a level spot with an amazing view and work on your favourite poses. Choose poses that aid relaxation and focus, and let the natural surroundings do the rest.

- Complete beginners can try the simple yoga pose opposite, known as the mountain pose. Its simplicity belies its power – it's a basic pose but there's a lot going on. This standing-up pose can improve posture and balance, help with sciatica, reduce stress and improve breathing technique.

The Mountain Pose (Tadasana)

- Stand with feet hip-width apart. Lift your toes to make sure your weight is distributed evenly over the four corners of your feet, then relax your toes back down to the ground.

- Engage the muscles in your calves and thighs and lift your body from the crown of your head. The crown of your head is the top of the mountain.

- Open your shoulders and lift your spine. Your arms should be positioned by your sides with palms facing your thighs.

- Draw in your navel and tuck in your tailbone. Your head should be centred over your heart and your heart over your pelvis. Draw energy up through your body from your heels to the crown of your head.

- Your throat should be soft, and the tongue wide and flat on the floor of your mouth. Soften your eyes and hold the pose for 30 seconds to 1 minute, breathing steadily.

~~~~~~~~~~~~~~~

Breathing Exercise From an Olympian

When I spoke with Olympian snowboarder and Doctor of Traditional Chinese Medicine Dominique Vallée (*see* page 62), I asked her for an activity that she would recommend to her patients to beat stress and anxiety (which she sees a lot of, even in Whistler, British Columbia, a place of such mountain-fired bliss).

'One thing I always focus on in treatment is regular deep yoga belly breathing. I think most of us after childhood forget how to breathe properly and only do upper chest breathing and this can bring in nervousness, stress and anxiety. If you look at babies when they breathe, their bellies are so big and round – you should put your hands on your stomach and make sure your belly really pushes out.'

To practice deep abdominal breathing, sit or stand in a comfortable position and close your eyes.

1. Inhale through your nose slowly and deeply for a count of five

2. Hold the breath for a count of five, or as long as is comfortable

3. Exhale slowly and smoothly through your mouth for a count of five

'Not only do you use 100 per cent of your lungs instead of 50–70 per cent, it forces you to calm down your nervous system, helps with digestion and absorption, helps with sleep, and is just a good overall full-body decompressor,' Dominique explained.

~~~~~~~~~~~~~~~

Awe-Inspiring Activities

Experiencing awe is beneficial to our mental health (*see* page 45). Recent studies have shown a connection between the experience of awe and improved creativity and problem solving, improved health, and an increase in social behaviours such as kindness, cooperation and sharing.[46]

Awe occurs when we experience something extraordinary, which challenges our understanding of the world; we experience awe in the face of beauty, great skill, virtue or natural phenomena, such as watching water tumble over an impressive waterfall or hearing thunder in a forceful storm. Awe can have elements of gratitude, admiration, wonder and love, but also fear and dread as we can infer from the words 'awesome' and 'awful'.

Awe can affect us deeply because it encourages us to step out of ourselves and reconsider what we know about the world, leading to personal growth and a reassessment of our values and our place in the world. To experience awe, we need to seek out experiences that will give us goosebumps, and mountain areas are the perfect places to find them.

- STAR-GAZING – the lack of light pollution in mountain regions makes them ideal for star-gazing. Choose a clear night and take a picnic blanket and flask with you. Lay back and wonder at the sheer vastness of the universe – even the mountains will feel small in comparison.

- MOUNTAIN WATERFALLS AND LAKES – natural scenes of beauty can inspire awe, as can those we find mildly threatening. Seek out beautiful mountain lakes or thundering waterfalls and hike out to visit them. Studies have shown that being close to water has a relaxing effect on us, too, so there is a lot to gain here.

- VISITING GEOLOGICAL FEATURES – giant rock faces, deep caves, steep valleys and craggy pinnacles can make us gasp in wonder, so it's well worth finding some awe-inspiring features to visit. A view from a mountain top will offer the same effect, especially if you have climbed up there yourself.

Energetic Activities

On top of the relaxation effects of spending time in a natural setting, and the feelings of awe inspired by the landscape, taking part in energetic activities in the mountains – such as hiking, skiing or climbing – can offer all the added benefits of physical exercise. Even a brisk walk will improve your mood due to the release of happy hormones endorphins into the bloodstream, and result in better sleep.

Staying Safe

By their very nature, mountain landscapes pose an element of risk to those engaged in activities that take them off the beaten track. Weather can change quickly and without warning and it's more difficult to get help if you need it. To stay safe in the mountains:

- Choose trails or routes that are suitable for your level of fitness

- Inform family or friends of your route and your expected finish date

- If you're planning to visit a remote region, consider investing in a GPS device that will track your route. You can also share your route in real time with family and friends, or send an emergency message if required

- Bring either a waterproof topographical map of your route, or use a pre-downloaded map app on your phone, so that you don't have to rely on signal

- Pack non-perishable food and as much water as you can comfortably carry

- Warm, waterproof and lightweight outerwear technology has come a long way in recent years: pack extra layers

Access to the Countryside Inspires Conservation

Recreational activities such as hiking and climbing help connect people with the natural environment. The need to respect and preserve our wild places can be better understood by exploring and enjoying the landscape in question. The UK government has recognized the importance of public access to the countryside as a means of reconnecting people with the natural environment, stating that 'a healthy, properly functioning natural environment is the foundation of sustained economic growth, prospering communities and personal wellbeing,' and that 'everyone should have fair access to a good-quality natural environment.'

The National Ecosystem Assessment estimates the social benefits of accessing the countryside to be £484 million ($630 million) per year. And without access, people are less likely to be motivated to conserve the landscapes.

Hiking and Hillwalking

Some people enjoy hiking in its own right, for others it is a means of getting out into the countryside and experiencing the mountains up close. Walking is one of the easiest ways of exercising – you can do it just about anywhere and it requires no special equipment – but walking in a beautiful natural setting brings a range of emotional health benefits too (*see* pages 34 and 68).

Skiing and Snowboarding

Skiing or snowboarding at a resort offers an excess of thrills and exercise and is probably the quickest way to experience a mountain in winter. For a more untamed adventure, consider hitting the backcountry at a heli-ski or cat-ski operation, where a professional guide will take you to otherwise inaccessible wilderness regions.

Climbing

Climbing is the quintessential mountain activity and one that engenders a deep connection with the mountains through direct hand-to-rock contact. If you've never tried it before, it's best to join a climbing club or go with a guide to learn the basic skills and find an achievable route on which you can experience some safe and enjoyable climbing. See pages 34 and 68 for the physical and emotional benefits climbing can offer.

High-Altitude Breathing

If you are exercising at high altitude, you might find you are short of breath. This is because barometric pressure decreases the higher you go, resulting in less oxygen entering your lungs as you breathe. You will probably find you start to breathe faster to bring in more oxygen, but there are two breathing techniques you can try to work with your lungs rather than against them.

Deep breathing
Slow down your breathing rate, but increase the depth of your breaths. Breathe slowly and deeply, inhaling until your belly expands. As your activity increases, increase the frequency of your breaths, but keep inhaling as deeply as possible.

Pressure breathing
Purse your lips and forcefully exhale. This technique removes greater amounts of carbon dioxide, providing a better environment for oxygen exchange in your lungs.

Ideally, you should slow your pace or reduce exertion to keep your breathing at a level that will allow you to continue to exercise, instead of pausing for breath.

How to Travel to High Altitude

Last Frontier Heliskiing is well-named. It really is a 'frontier' in the definitive sense of the word, which is 'the extreme limit of settled land beyond which lies wilderness', according to the *Oxford Dictionary of English*. The helicopter skiing outfit's enormous tenure – about the size of the main island of Hawaii – lies in the Skeena and Coast Mountain ranges of northern British Columbia near the Alaskan border.

Last Frontier Heliskiing's Director of Operations, Cliff Umpleby, is the guy who makes sure everyone is guided safely and effectively through this trackless maze of alpine bowls, glaciers and forests – the fevered dream of any big-mountain skier. In addition to his position at Last Frontier Heliskiing, Umpleby guides clients on backcountry ski-touring and mountaineering trips and also frequently tours with friends. He has summited Mount Logan in the southwestern Yukon three times, including one expedition that lasted 27 days. I asked him to take us behind the scenes of climbing and skiing Canada's highest mountain (and at 5,959 metres (19,500 feet) the second-highest in North America). How badly does Logan beat up a ski mountaineer?

'Due to the altitude and cold, we take a whole lot of gear with us,' he said. 'One day we'll climb up to an area where we're going to make camp, leave a cache of food and equipment, come back down, and spend the night at lower altitude. The next day we would pack up all the gear and move it up to where we had cached, then set up camp there. Slowly but surely we worked our way higher and higher up the mountain until we were in a position to go for the summit.'

Even with all this planning to avoid the worst effects of high altitude on the body, Umpleby has not always been spared. 'I've had Acute Mountain Sickness (AMS) a few times. As you're moving gradually higher up the mountain those symptoms will get worse to the point where you get into camp feeling sick. The only thing that stops your raging headache is literally not to move. And as soon as you start moving around, you feel extreme shortness of breath, debilitating headaches and often nausea. The only way to fight that is to just lay there and do nothing, or go back down to a lower altitude.

'What we'll do as a rule of thumb is to ascend maybe 600 metres (2,000 feet) and see what happens. Typically those symptoms will go away, but if they persist, you might have to drop lower. Let's say you get ill at around 4,000 metres (13,100 feet) and then you drop back to, say, just above 3,000 metres (9,800 feet) and then if you go back up and you're feeling good, that might be it. You never feel 100 per cent, but it never really sets into that debilitating feeling again...Almost every time there's some altitude-related issue. Probably some of that is just finding your pace with the people you're with. So if you go too high, too fast, you're going to get ill. You have to listen to your body and pace yourself appropriately.'

When he and a few friends climbed Mont Blanc (pictured opposite) a few years ago, Umpleby observed the wrong way to ascend to high altitude. 'To climb Mont Blanc, a lot of people take the Aiguille du Midi cable car from Chamonix. So people come from fairly low altitudes up very high, very fast and get to a hut [Refuge des Cosmiques]. When we walked into the hut there was a whole line of people overhanging the balcony, throwing up. But we had started in Chamonix and walked and climbed the entire way, doing a bunch of smaller subsidiary peaks on the way up to Blanc. We did the whole trip without using cable cars.'

CHAPTER 6

BRINGING THE MOUNTAINS CLOSER TO HOME

~~~~~~~~

"Somewhere between the
bottom of the climb and
the summit is the answer to
the mystery why we climb."

— Greg Child

Most of us have less leisure time than we'd like and little access to the mountains, so is there any way we can bring the benefits of the mountains closer to home? One simple way is to use a mountain scene as a screensaver on your computer, or hang photographs of mountains on the walls. Studies show that just looking at still images of nature can lower our stress levels in the same way as being actually there,[47] so perhaps we can also experience awe (*see* page 45) without leaving home.

Virtual reality is another way we can experience a mountain setting in our own homes. Virtual reality (VR) is a three-dimensional, computer-generated simulation of an environment which we can interact with and explore. There are several mountain experiences available, including a simulated trek to the top of Everest, with all the feelings of awe and exhilaration it entails.

Virtual reality is becoming increasing popular in healthcare settings and therapists are using virtual scenes of nature – forests, coastal areas and so on – for their calming properties as a treatment for mental fatigue, stress and anxiety. These treatments are particularly valuable to those who cannot access such restorative natural places for themselves, perhaps because they have limited mobility or live in a care home.

~~~~~~~~~~

Mountain Fitness at Home

Many mountain activities can be enjoyed closer to where you live.

• Outdoor exercise in a natural setting such as a park will offer the same wellbeing benefits wherever you are. Physical activity in nature is a powerful stress-buster and you are more likely to exercise harder outside (*see* page 35).

• Recreate the terrain of the mountains by forgoing the level paths and exercising in woodland or on hilly ground. Uneven ground is good for balance and flexibility, and uphill stretches increase the cardiovascular workout.

• Experience climbing in a controlled and safe setting at one of the many indoor and outdoor climbing walls. Enhance your strength, endurance and flexibility while fostering a keen sense of achievement and problem solving.

• Try skiing or snowboarding on a dry slope or indoor snow slope. These fast-paced activities provide a full-body workout, improve coordination and joint tensility and can sharpen the mind due to the quick decision-making required (*see* page 69).

~~~~~~~~~~

A Mountain Visualization

Visualization is a method of guided relaxation that can have a profound effect on the body, mind and emotions, reducing stress, improving memory and aiding good sleep. The idea is to turn your awareness inwards and use your imagination to visualize a mountain scene and reap all the emotional benefits you would gain if you were really there.

- Choose a quiet place where you can rest undisturbed for 20–30 minutes. Make yourself as comfortable as possible lying on your back. Support your head with a cushion and raise your knees off the floor with a rolled-up blanket. Cover yourself with a light blanket unless the room is very warm.

- Close your eyes and bring your attention to the flow of your breathing. Feel each breath as it comes in and out, just observing it without trying to change it.

- Picture in your mind's eye the most beautiful mountain you can. It might be a mountain you know, or one from your imagination. Hold the image and feeling of this mountain, letting it gradually come into greater focus. Examine its overall shape, its peak high in the sky, its base rooted in the rock of the earth's crust. Does it have just one peak or is made up of a series of peaks or a high plateau? Notice whether the sides are steep or gently sloping. Notice how massive the mountain is, how solid and unmoving, how beautiful. Feel the sense of awe at its presence.

- Now zoom in and start to notice some of the features of the mountain. Is there snow on the mountain, are there areas of forest? Can you see any bare rock?

- Come closer still and envisage a rocky outcrop. Imagine sitting on the rocks and looking around you. What colour are the rocks? Can you feel the texture of the rock through your clothes? Try to fill in as much detail as you can, using as many senses as possible.

- Feel the cool breeze on your face and smell the fresh mountain air. Feel the sun warming your skin and enjoy the calming sense of wellbeing and relaxation. Stay here for as long as you can, savouring the remoteness of the setting.

Mountain Tea

People living in the mountains of Greece, Turkey, Albania, Kosovo, Bulgaria and Macedonia have long been collecting a herb, *Sideritis scardica* (also known as ironwort), to be enjoyed as a herbal tea. Since antiquity, this mountain tea has been used as a kind of panacea to treat all manner of conditions. It is reputed to aid digestion, boost the immune system, protect against colds, flu and other viruses, treat allergies, shortness of breath and sinus congestion, even reduce pain and anxiety.

Recent scientific studies have shown that these claims about the curative properties of mountain tea may have some basis in fact. Mountain tea is known to have antimicrobial and antioxidant properties and significant research has confirmed its ability to prevent colds, flu and allergies. One study showed potent anti-inflammatory and gastroprotective activities of the herb, as well as promising anti-cancer properties.[48]

Mountain tea has also long been used to treat age-related problems in the elderly, including the symptoms of Alzheimer's disease. A 2016 study suggests that extracts of this plant could be used to treat cognitive impairment and decline in the elderly.[49]

Mountain tea is readily available to buy online and has a sweet, floral and earthy flavour. It can be enjoyed with honey, cinnamon or lemon.

Edelweiss

Edelweiss (*Leontopodium nivale*) (pictured right) is another mountain plant whose benefits can be enjoyed anywhere. Native to the Pyrénées, the Alps and mountain regions in the Balkans, Edelweiss grows on limey soils in stony meadows at altitudes of 1,000–3,500 metres (3,300–11,500 feet). It has distinctive white flowers and silver foliage with dense hair, which appears to protect the plant from cold, aridity and ultraviolet radiation.

Traditionally, extracts of the plant have been used to treat abdominal disorders, angina and other heart conditions, bronchitis, rheumatism, fever, dysentery and many other complaints, but today it's the plant's antioxidant properties which are attracting interest from the skin care industry. Edelweiss contains high concentrations of leontopodic acids which have strong antioxidant properties, and exhibits strong anti-collagenase and hyaluronidase properties, limiting the degradation of important macromolecules in the skin.

An anti-aging ingredient has been developed using edelweiss stem cells which harnesses the protective substances the plant uses to defend itself against the harsh climate in which it lives. Edelweiss is being incorporated into anti-aging creams, sunscreens and serums by cosmetics companies around the world. Edelweiss has many components that could potentially create younger-looking skin, protecting cells and preventing the breakdown of collagen associated with aging.

Essential Oils from the Mountains

Essential oils are natural aromatic compounds found in the leaves, seeds, flowers and stems of plants and offer one of the easiest ways to introduce the benefits of mountain plants into your home. Scientific research has shown that inhaling essential oils can have a physiological relaxation effect on the body, lowering blood pressure, increasing activity in the parasympathetic nervous system (known to increase during relaxation) and calming activity in the prefrontal area of the brain.[50] These effects only occur, however, when you like the aroma you are inhaling: so be sure to choose something you find pleasant.

- Add a few drops of essential oil to a warm bath and lie back to enjoy the aroma.

- Place a few drops of a calming essential oil such as lavender on your pillowcase or a tissue next to your pillow to aid good sleep.

- Use an essential oil diffuser to scent a room.

- Mix a little essential oil with a massage oil for a therapeutic massage.

- Mix with water in a simple spray bottle and mist over carpets or clean laundry.

HIMALAYAN CEDAR

Himalayan Cedar (*Cedrus deodara*) is a high mountain tree growing at altitudes of 1,000–3,000 metres (3,300–9,900 feet) in the Himalayas. The oil derived from the wood has long been used in Ayurvedic medicine to treat a wide range of ailments, from fevers and dysentery to bronchitis and even snake bites. The resin is used to treat bruises, joint injuries and skin diseases, while the leaves are used in the treatment of tuberculosis.

The essential oil has a strong, dry, woody aroma. It is slightly smoky and balsamic with a hint of spice. Inhalation can help support a healthy respiratory system, especially during the winter months. It can be added to skin-care products to help neutralize oily skin, or used in a diffuser to balance emotions.

HIGH ALPINE LAVENDER

High alpine lavender (*Lavandula angustifolia*) grows wild in rocky, mountainous areas. The thin air and sunshine at high altitude produce a higher concentration of aromatic compounds, intensifying its unique aroma and therapeutic benefits.

Lavender has been used for thousands of years in cosmetics, medicine and perfumes. Lavender oil was used in Ancient Greece and Rome to disinfect sick rooms and clean wounds. The Romans scented their baths with lavender and in fact the name derives from the Latin *lavare*, meaning 'to wash'.

Lavender essential oil has a soothing fragrance, sweet and flowery with woody undertones. It is most appreciated for its calming and relaxing properties and is commonly used as an antidote to stress and insomnia, or by those suffering from depression, anxiety, mood swings or irritability. It is also used as a natural antiseptic for

soothing insect bites, burns and acne. Add a few drops to a soothing warm bath before bedtime to relax and calm the mind, inducing a peaceful night's sleep.

ANDEAN MINT

Andean Mint or muña (*Minthostachys setosa*) is a multi-branched, small-leaved deciduous shrub native to the high Peruvian Andes (pictured), prized for its medicinal and aromatic properties. The herb is used locally as a condiment in cooking, as a tea to treat digestive problems and respiratory conditions, and is also believed to keep bones and teeth healthy.

Andean mint essential oil has a fresh, bright, penetrating mint scent due to its high menthol content. It is effective as a remedy for colds, reducing mucous and fever and encouraging perspiration. It has cooling and pain-relieving properties which seem to ease headaches, migraines and toothache.

It has a soothing effect on the digestive system and can be used to treat travel sickness, vomiting, diarrhoea and constipation – use one drop on a sugar cube or mix with a teaspoon of honey. The oil can be used externally for the relief of muscle aches, joint pain and bruising.

PINK PEPPER

Peruvian Pink Pepper or molle (*Schinus molle*) is an evergreen tree which grows wild in the Peruvian Andes. The ancient Incas revered the tree and indigenous peoples have long valued its astringent, diuretic and antiviral properties to treat a wide range of medical conditions, including colds, flu, asthma, bronchitis and other respiratory problems, hypertension and heart arrhythmia, as well as menstrual disorders and symptoms of menopause.

The essential oil is extracted from the seeds of the tree – what we know in cookery as pink peppercorns – and has a fresh peppery aroma with fruity and floral undertones. It can be used internally to treat digestive problems, soothing an upset stomach, clearing digestive infections and stimulating slow digestion. Use externally to treat sprains, arthritis and muscular aches and stiffness. Inhale the aroma to reduce stress and fatigue, energizing the mind and the emotions. Avoid using it just before bed as its stimulative effects will encourage wakefulness.

Plant a Mountain Tree

Another way to bring the mountains closer to home is the simple act of planting a tree, one of the many species that thrive at higher altitude but may be grown in many climate zones. Conservationist John Muir (*see page 72*) always paid close attention to trees as he climbed and wandered in the Sierra and other ranges, and relished sleeping rough in groves of sugar pine. 'Even the blind must enjoy these woods,' he wrote in his 1901 book *Our National Parks*, describing a walk in Yosemite, 'drinking their fragrance, listening to the music of the winds in their groves, and fingering their flowers and plumes and cones and richly furrowed boles. The kind of study required is as easy and natural as breathing. Without any great knowledge of botany or wood-craft, in a single season you may learn the name and something more of nearly every kind of tree in the park.'

One tree particularly evocative of mountains, and celebrated by Muir, is the incense cedar (*Calocedrus decurrens*). It grows in the mixed conifer forests of the Sierra Nevada and the Cascade Mountains as well as coastal ranges, western Nevada, and as far south as Baja, northwestern Mexico. With scaly, red-brown bark, a mature tree is broadly conical with a full crown. In the Sierra the tree can reach 30–45 metres (100–150 feet) and live over a thousand years. In cultivation, it grows 9–15 metres (30–50 feet) When crushed, the foliage emits a lingering, incense-like scent.

Here is Muir's typically detailed description of the tree:

'Another conifer was met to-day – incense cedar...a large tree with warm yellow-green foliage in flat plumes like those of arborvitae, bark cinnamon-colored, and as the boles of the old trees are without limbs they make striking pillars in the woods where the sun chances to shine on them – a worthy companion of the kingly sugar and yellow pines. I feel strangely attracted to this tree. The brown close-grained wood, as well as the small scale-like leaves, is fragrant, and the flat overlapping plumes make fine beds, and must shed the rain well. It would be delightful to be storm-bound beneath one of these noble, hospitable, inviting old trees, its broad sheltering arms bent down like a tent, incense rising from the fire made from its dry fallen branches, and a hearty wind chanting overhead.'

Who wouldn't want to bring a touch of that into their own backyard?

CHAPTER 7

THE FUTURE FOR MOUNTAIN RESEARCH AND CONSERVATION

~~~~~~~~~~

"The mountains are calling
and I must go."

— John Muir

So how does the future look for our precious mountain regions around the world? The following pages discuss some of the current areas of research as well as a few of the conservation initiatives set up to protect these places, so vital to human life and wellbeing.

Research into High-Altitude Genetics

Cynthia Beall is a physical anthropologist and professor at Case Western Reserve University in Cleveland, Ohio, who has studied genetic adaptations to high altitude around the world, focusing on indigenous populations in East Africa, the Andes and Tibet. While typical lowlanders become debilitatingly short of breath if they ascend quickly to high altitude, long-settled populations such as highlander Tibetans, whose ancestors have been living at altitude for 11,000 years, do not. Over a long period, this isolated population has experienced natural selection.

Beall's research has focused on the exact nature of these high-altitude adaptations, and how and why the Tibetans' blood flow increases at higher elevation. They exhale excessive amounts of the gas nitric oxide, Beall and her colleagues discovered, helping their blood vessels stay relaxed.[51] And in contrast to populations in the high Andes, Tibetans do not have higher levels of hemoglobin, the oxygen-carrying molecules. Tibetans' enhanced blood flow at altitude may instead be due to a gene they carry known as EPAS1. They inherited this gene from an obscure branch of hominid, known as Denisovans, who around 50,000 years ago lived in the mountainous region of what is now Siberia. This long-developing genetic adaptation allows them to avoid much of the hypoxia that afflicts lowlanders when they ascend above 3,500 metres (11,500 feet).

Understanding the genetics behind the high-altitude adaptations that allow certain populations to beat hypoxia (by effectively delivering oxygen throughout their bodies) can be applied to people everywhere who suffer from conditions that cause hypoxia, including heart disease.[52] 'You may be surprised to learn that something like 30 per cent of deaths in the US are associated with hypoxia,' Beall said.

SECRETS OF THE SHERPA

In a related research development, the University of British Columbia recently mounted an international expedition to study the Sherpa of the Khumbu region of Nepal (pictured), who are famed for their climbing prowess and functionality at high altitude. Sherpas' distinctive gene pool – that may hold the secrets of their superior high-altitude adaptation – is in danger of loss through migration and urbanization, so immediate study is of urgent importance. The expedition aimed to discover the physiological differences between Sherpa and lowlanders in their various responses to sustained high-altitude exposure at 5,050 metres (16,600 feet) of elevation. Michael Tymko is a Ph.D candidate at the University of British Columbia's School of Health and Exercise Sciences and was a co-author of the study overview published in late 2018.[53] I asked Tymko how this study's initial results might be applied generally.

'Ways to apply results from these expeditions are multifaceted,' he said, 'with implications for military deployment to high altitude (for example Afghanistan), for the growing numbers of lowlanders vacationing at high-altitude destinations, and for commercial flight personnel who are exposed to mild levels of hypoxia during flight. The data that we collect can have direct translational impact for patients in critical care and in other conditionals that are characterized by hypoxia (for example lung disease, heart failure, sepsis). Beyond these translational aspects of our work, a big motivator for these expeditions is mainly based on scientific curiosity.

'In my opinion, from an evolutionary perspective, it is incredibly cool that there are populations at altitude that have evolved to perform better than other populations. The holy grail for high altitude research is whether there is a way to "predict" those who are prone to altitude sickness prior to their ascent to altitude. As of now, despite stacks of research, there are no clear predictors for altitude illness in healthy humans (age, sex, race, fitness and so on). Perhaps the answers to this question (and other questions) are hidden within the physiology of these unique high-altitude populations.'

The study's results are complex and will be revealed in research papers to be published over several years, but Tymko summarized some initial findings as follows:

- Sherpa have faster muscle recovery at altitude compared to lowlanders.

- Peripheral blood vessel function is maintained in Sherpa, but reduced in lowlanders, when ascending to high altitude.

- Sherpa seem to have different autonomic (nervous) regulation compared to lowlanders at high altitude.

I asked Tymko for his anecdotal impressions of the Sherpa. 'The Sherpa, in general, are a very tranquil and happy population,' he said. 'They don't make much money, maybe the equivalent of $5–10 USD per day, but they are very content with living simple, quiet lives, and have a broad network of friends and family across the many high-altitude villages in the Khumbu valley. They love the mountains. One of my colleagues asked one of the local Sherpa we were working with: "Would you move somewhere else to make more money?", and his response was "Why would I move? I live in the most beautiful place in the world."'

A New Model of Conservation: Yellowstone to Yukon

'What we have in the Rocky Mountains is rare – an almost complete representation of all native large mammals that roamed the great hills before Europeans arrived. From the perspective of the great mountain ecosystems of the world, it's the last of the last.'
– Dr Paul Paquet, Scientist with the World Wildlife Fund

As human populations continue to grow, urban development fans in haphazard fashion ever outward from city and town centres, heedless of the habitat swallowed up and fragmented in the process. Perhaps the general idea behind national parks has always included the preservation of habitat within one watershed or mountain range. But due to the demands of private property and extractive industries, most national parks are hard-won silos protecting cultural or natural heritage from alteration, but abutted by agricultural or industrialized land, highways, cities and towns. A newer model of conservation aims to expand ecological integrity across larger, connected sections of land, even spanning international borders.

Since 1993, the Yellowstone to Yukon Conservation Initiative (Y2Y), has promoted this model. Y2Y is a US-Canada not-for-profit initiative, designed to connect and conserve habitat from Yellowstone National Park (in Wyoming, with smaller sections in Montana and Idaho) to Canada's far-northwest Yukon Territory. This is a vast and varied ecosystem spanning thousands of kilometres of mountains, meadows, foothills, plains, old-growth temperate inland forests, scrubland, wetlands, and innumerable lakes and rivers. At over 3,200km (2,000 miles) in length, the Y2Y region is, in spite of centuries of settlement and development, still mostly intact. It includes the Rocky Mountains and lesser ranges and is, as Dr Paul Paquet's quote above suggests, a stronghold for big mammals including moose, elk, caribou, lynx, wolverine, wolf and bear. The Y2Y organization approaches conservation collaboratively, working with over 300 landowners, businesses, government agencies, conservation groups, donors, First Nations communities and scientists.

CONNECTING LANDSCAPES

Dr Jodi Hilty, Y2Y's President and Chief Scientist, is an ecologist who specializes in studying and maintaining wildlife corridors. 'I love the idea of a connected landscape,' said Hilty, 'and Y2Y is one of the oldest and most well-known large landscape visions. It's an old enough movement that they've been able to both qualitatively and quantitatively demonstrate that having a large vision and working across so many groups can have an impact. There's a document [released on Y2Y's 20th anniversary in 2013] called *20 Years of Progress* that to me was the game-changer: they were able to show significant increase in protected areas, from 11 to 21 per cent. Today there are 105 crossing structures, overpasses and underpasses dedicated solely to wildlife. We have work to do in some places, but that's really tangible progress towards this vision of "connect and protect" for the whole landscape, for both people and nature.'

With such an enormous working area, I asked Hilty how she decides what to focus on. 'There are lots of groups working across the Y2Y region, and then there's the organization that I oversee,' she explained. 'Within the organization, we focus on areas where there is an enormous need and opportunity to create protected areas, for example the Peace River Break area [in northeastern British Columbia].' The Peace River Break is not only the narrowest part of the Yellowstone-to-Yukon corridor, it is also the narrowest section of the Rocky Mountains. 'For decades it has been British Columbia's environmental sacrificial lamb,' said Tim Burkhart, Y2Y's Peace Region Coordinator. 'While other parts of the province have seen development balanced with conservation, the Peace has rampant industrial development in the form of oil and gas, shale gas, coalbed methane and mining, wind farms and dams, which is changing this into a highly industrialized landscape.'[54]

Hilty added: 'The Peace River Break is only four per cent protected so it's obvious that from our perspective we've got a lot of work to do in that region...we've been working with a variety of partners, including the Treaty 8 First Nations. One of the caribou populations has disappeared and most of the remaining populations are declining by 10–50 per cent a year. It's a tough situation because of the cumulative impacts of human developments of different kinds across the landscape. Collectively we want to see that landscape rebalanced. It doesn't mean no [resource] extraction. It just means there are places that we need to look at restoring and protecting so that there's a chance that ecosystem can rebound over the long term.'

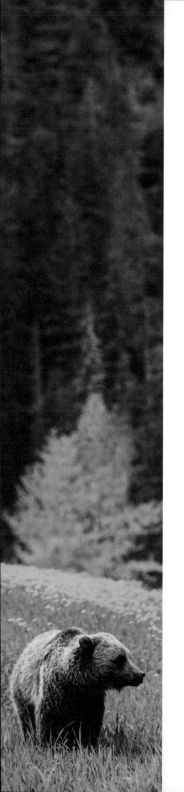

Grizzlies on the Border

Jodi Hilty pinpoints the mountainous Canada-US border section of the Y2Y region as a major focus for her work, since the landscape here is deeply fragmented. 'There are places along the border where recent work on a number of different species has shown fragmentation from a genetics perspective – animals that were once a continuous population are now in sub-populations,' Hilty said. One of those species is grizzly bear (*Ursus arctos horribilis*, a subspecies of brown bear). Y2Y has relied on the work of wildlife biologist Dr Michael Proctor, who has studied grizzlies since the mid-1990s and focuses his research on the population on the southern Selkirk and Purcell Ranges, lately under pressure from new roads and agriculture.

Y2Y and Proctor zoned in on the Cabinet-Purcell Mountain Corridor, linking the Cabinet Mountains south of the international border to habitat to the north, tracking grizzlies with radio collars. By monitoring grizzly movement, Y2Y can then allocate resources appropriately. 'We just let the bears teach us where they're crossing these highways,' said Proctor. 'And so far that's been pretty successful.' The author of many papers on these apex predators – North America's second-largest land carnivore after the polar bear – Proctor has also drafted a map for Y2Y outlining the critical zones near the border where habitat is severely impacted. 'Over the last ten years we've largely secured three of the really narrow bottleneck corridors between otherwise isolated populations of grizzly bear,' said Hilty. 'We worked with a variety of US and Canadian land trusts to purchase those pieces…and we are now working towards a restoration of those lands.'

I asked Hilty if a species such as grizzly bear would potentially exhibit more threatening behaviour due to climate change. Her answer points to the importance of connected landscapes. 'When we have dry, hot years and berry crops fail or we have poor whitebark pine production, grizzly bears (being generalists and opportunists) will seek other food sources and that means they have to move across the landscape. So bears are going to lower elevation, often private land in valley bottoms, and that's where we see an increase in potential conflicts if those communities don't have strong coexistence practices.'

PROTECTING VULNERABLE ECOSYSTEMS

Is there one part of the Yellowstone-to-Yukon region, I asked Hilty, that is more vulnerable to climate change – or is the whole region equally vulnerable? 'There's a couple of ways that I would answer that,' Hilty said. 'One is to look back at history in places like the McKenzie Mountains and the Columbia Headwaters – past *refugia* during times of climate change – and say we might want to pay more attention to those places. The flip side of that is to look at what's most imperilled: places with local stressors, meaning generally increased human activities, where a watershed has already been heavily impacted. These systems are a lot more vulnerable to climate change. And what we do is work at different scales. At the coarsest scale, if you look at the climate science, Y2Y is a response to climate change. Mountain systems can help during climate change by giving species the opportunity to adapt. They don't have to move as far to find different micro-climates; they can go up in elevation and they can go to different slopes and aspects. And Y2Y is also a north-south chain for animals who might be moving more northerly.

BUILDING RESILIENCE TO CLIMATE CHANGE

'The higher you go in the alpine systems, the more vulnerable they are. It's my hope that these systems are able to maintain their ecological function, whether that's maintaining forests against fires and floods, or predator-prey dynamics, that all helped to shape what this place is. This doesn't mean kicking people out, it just means human activities being sensitive to the fragility of the ecosystem and not impairing it in a permanent way.

'And at a coarser scale our work is about reducing stressors. We have a project on the border of British Columbia in the Idaho Panhandle to do restoration work on a wetland which is a known landscape-level corridor – last summer we saw a collared grizzly bear move right through that area. This is hugely important for local biodiversity and endemic animals. So we're trying to address those areas that have been heavily human-impacted but in some cases can be restored to be a little bit more resilient to climate change. We also spend time trying to shift the global paradigm from just protected areas which are hugely important but aren't going to be adequate to conserve global biodiversity. We have to start working on a connected landscape scale.'

As examples, Hilty mentioned several large-scale habitat connectivity efforts inspired by Y2Y, including the Baja to Bering Marine Priority Conservation Area (B2B) which is an attempt to link the corridors and coastline from the tropical east Pacific off Mexico to the Arctic Ocean, and also Australia's Great Eastern Ranges Initiative (GER) linking 3,600km (2,200 miles) of montane habitat from western Victoria through New South Wales to northern Queensland.

WHY CONNECTED LANDSCAPES MATTER

What if, I asked Hilty, you were talking to somebody who didn't know anything about biodiversity and didn't live in the region, who asked: 'Why should I care about the Yellowstone-to-Yukon Conservation Initiative?'

'I would tell them that the Yellowstone to Yukon region is globally significant because it's one of the most intact mountain systems in the world. We're seeing millions of people every year coming from all over the world to see and enjoy this place. There are also practical reasons: this region is the headwaters for water that at least 15 million people use and it's also the natural filtration and storage system for that water. Not to mention all the other kinds of natural services that we get just from having nature out there doing a job for free that would otherwise be really expensive to recreate using engineering.'

Hilty also pointed out the lifestyle benefits of the region. 'We can look a little bit further south in the Rockies to Colorado and over the last number of years they've come to realize that nature is one of their highest values and they're really focusing on conserving and restoring it. That's also true around Yellowstone. And we're seeing businesses saying they're going to move their headquarters to somewhere in the Y2Y, and advertising jobs with the quality of life as a component explicitly written into those jobs. And I think we will see more of this as people realize the value of these spaces.'

~~~~~~~~~~

Connecting Europe's Bone-Breakers

Two hundred years ago, lammergeyers (*Gypaetus barbatus*, also known as bearded vultures, pictured opposite) were found in all mountain regions across southern Europe, from western Spain to the Balkans. Today these majestic raptors are highly endangered, partly due to a decrease in the availability of food, partly due to changes in animal husbandry, but also because of the bird's bad reputation. In the past, people thought lammergeyers killed lambs and sometimes even children so these vultures were hunted down. In the Alps, there was a bounty for each animal killed, so they became extinct there in 1913.

However, lammergeyers do not hunt live prey. The majority of their diet consists of bleached bones from ibex, chamois and deer carcasses. The bird can swallow bones the size of a sheep's vertebrae. If bones are too big, they carry them high into the sky and drop them on to rocks below from a height of up to 100 meters (330 feet) to shatter them, earning them the name of 'Bone-breaker'. This unique habit of recycling makes lammergeyers an important part of the ecosystem.

Today lammergeyers occur only in the Pyrénées, with tiny populations in the mountains of Crete and Corsica, and a small reintroduced population in the Alps. A conservation project has been set up to connect the new Alpine population with that in the Pyrénées. The Life Gypconnect program aims to reintroduce the species to the Massif Central mountains in France, lying midway between the Pyrénées and Alps, to establish a corridor and foster exchanges between the two populations, contributing to their sustainability.[55]

~~~~~~~~~~

PRESSURES FROM DEVELOPMENT

How does the Yellowstone to Yukon Conservation Initiative (*see* page 160) deal with development pressures from deep-pocketed mining or oil and gas interests? 'Extractive industries are one of the many human activities that happen across the region,' Jodi Hilty (*see* page 161) said. 'We're really fortunate that many people across this community really do value nature. We don't win because we have billions of dollars. We win because we are able to mobilize the hearts of so many people who also care about this place. And sometimes that's even the companies themselves who voluntarily give up land or a concession because they know it's the right thing to do. Not everyone does that, but there are a number of examples of companies that act in really great ways.'

What's the end goal of Y2Y? 'We need to have core areas protected, and connectivity zones between them,' Hilty explained. 'The level of use by humans across all of those different designations has to be appropriate for a conservation today and for future generations. I would hazard to say all or almost all of this area is still under treaty rights for different Indigenous communities to hunt, fish and gather resources. And it will always be a used landscape. I think the question is, "How do we manage the cumulative impact of all the different uses, whether it's in parks, on private lands, or different kinds of designations, to ensure that the landscape can be a healthy, functional ecosystem for today and for future generations?"'

Human encroachment on wintering animals such as caribou – repeat helicopter flights over their habitat, for example – causes them to move more, use up their fat stores and may impede their ability to reproduce. 'We have to be sensitive to the fact that some of these species are hanging on quite precariously and humans in that system can have both subtle and profound impacts,' Hilty said. 'Higher elevations are more vulnerable to climate change, because [species] are trying to eke out a living in an already resource-poor environment with limited growing seasons.'

~~~~~~~~~~

Acquiring Darkwoods

Among others, one recent land conservation win inside the Y2Y region deserves a mention. What is now known as Darkwoods Conservation Area was, from 1967 until 2008, a 550-square kilometre (210-square mile) parcel of mountain wilderness in southeast British Columbia owned by Duke Carl Herzog von Württemberg of Germany. The Duke bought this thick slice of the Selkirk Range at the height of the Cold War as a refuge for his family in the event of a Soviet invasion of West Germany, and selectively logged the land – though never allowed clearcutting or hunting. In 2008, the Cold War over and the Duke now in his seventies, he was thinking about selling but wanted to keep the land he called Darkwoods (a nod to the Black Forest in his native land) intact and well-managed. He found a suitable buyer in the Nature Conservancy of Canada, and the subsequent transaction became the largest private conservation land sale in Canadian history.

In 2018 the Canadian federal government and the British Columbia provincial government announced funds towards the purchase of 79 square kilometres (30 square miles) to add to Darkwoods, in the Next Creek watershed, a key habitat of inland temperate rainforest. 'When they originally bought Darkwoods there was a sort of donut hole in the middle that wasn't conserved,' said Jodi Hilty. 'So they were able to complete the protection of that area. There was a transboundary caribou population here, which was the last herd in the US. It has functionally gone extinct: their count is down to three females, so short of immaculate conception, this herd is doomed. And that was due to intense logging in that region. So Darkwoods is one of the few core areas that remains. And my hope is that it's an anchor for landscape-level restoration in the future.'

~~~~~~~~~~

BIG-PICTURE BIODIVERSITY

Big-picture efforts such as the Y2Y aim to boost the biodiversity that our lives depend on, whether we're aware of it or not. According to the World Health Organization (WHO), 'Biodiversity loss can have significant direct human health impacts if ecosystem services are no longer adequate to meet social needs. Indirectly, changes in ecosystem services affect livelihoods, income, local migration and, on occasion, may even cause political conflict.' The WHO elaborates on further possible impacts to our health: 'Biophysical diversity of microorganisms, flora and fauna provides extensive knowledge which carries important benefits for biological, health, and pharmacological sciences... Loss in biodiversity may limit discovery of potential treatments for many diseases and health problems.' More immediate reasons to preserve global biodiversity can scarcely be imagined.

Biodiversity Hotspot: the Eastern Afromontane

Mountain or montane forests often contain rare species with distinct adaptations due to the elevation at which they live. The montane forest may not be as teeming in sheer numbers of species as a lowland tropical rainforest, but other factors – for example, geographical isolation – make moderate-altitude mountains keepers of biodiversity otherwise lost in more settled regions.

A good example is the *Eastern Afromontane*, a Biodiversity Hotspot as identified by Conservation International and the Critical Ecosystem Partnership Fund (CEPF). British biologist Norman Myers defined the hotspot as a place

of extraordinary species concentration – including large numbers of endemics (species not found anywhere else) – that is also threatened by human activity. The Eastern Afromontane is a far-flung series of mountains stretching from Saudi Arabia south to Zimbabwe and Mozambique, which are similar to one another geologically and biologically. The highest is Mount Kilimanjaro (5,895 metres/19,300 feet) but most peaks are much lower. The montane system contains a head-spinning array of variety, including pine, tropical broadleaf and bamboo forests, plus rare high-altitude wetlands and grasslands. To take just one example of incalculably valuable biodiversity found here, the Kafa Biosphere Reserve in southeastern Ethiopia harbours some of the last wild coffee forests (*Coffea arabica*) on earth.

The CEPF estimates that there are around 7,600 plant species in the Eastern Afromontane and at least 2,350 are endemic. These numbers will undoubtedly grow every year as studies continue and new species are discovered. CEPF also estimates the number of endemic mammals to be around a hundred, including the endangered Ethiopian wolf (*Canis simensis*) and the critically endangered mountain gorilla (*Gorilla beringei beringei*).

THE LIFE ZONE

In short, the Eastern Afromontane is not a Death Zone (the atmosphere above 8,000 metres/26,200 feet) but a 'Life Zone'. We'll take the recent conservation efforts on northern Mozambique's Mount Namuli, at the southern extent of the Afromontane, as an example of how it might be protected before population pressures permanently disrupt the ecosystem. The 2,419-metre (7,900-foot) Namuli is unlikely to be notched on any mountaineer's bedpost. As mountains go, it isn't extremely high or steep. The granite monolith can't boast an iconic horizon line like Argentina's Fitz Roy or Switzerland's

Matterhorn. If anything, it calls to mind the ruins of an ancient observatory looming above the surrounding rainforest and grassland, its summit often obscured by clouds. Like other peaks in the Afromontane, Namuli is an inselberg (from the German for 'island mountain'): an erosion-resistant geological relic older than (and towering above) the surrounding landscape and upon which flora and fauna live and evolve in relative isolation.

Namuli was effectively lost to the greater scientific and conservation community while civil war convulsed the region from the 1970s into the 1990s. Today, Mozambique's Zambezia province in which Namuli stands is peaceful, but the mountain and surroundings lack official conservation status.

REDISCOVERING LOST MOUNTAINS

Over the last few years, scientists and conservationists have set out to rediscover Namuli and nearby peaks, documenting many rare and threatened species. British botanist Jonathan Timberlake has been studying the flora of Mozambique and adjoining countries since the 1980s when he worked for the United Nations' Food and Agriculture Organization.

Later he undertook botanical surveys in the Eastern Afromontane, focusing on the forests and grasslands, for the Royal Botanical Gardens at Kew Herbarium – one of the world's largest collections of plant specimens, around 7 million and counting: an invaluable resource for studying the diversity of flora that keeps Earth green. Timberlake also led forestry research in Zimbabwe with a British Aid grant, and then for about ten years ran a non-governmental organization (NGO) documenting biodiversity across southern Africa.

'Mountains haven't been cleared to the same extent that the lowland areas have because people don't want

to live up there – it's too wet, or it's too cold, or it's too steep,' Timberlake explained. 'So mountains are refuges, though that's not to say they haven't been used or impacted – just much less than the surrounding lowlands.'

Armed with a Darwin Initiative grant, Timberlake and Dr Julian Bayliss from Oxford Brookes University in the UK undertook expeditions to Mount Namuli (pictured opposite) and nearby Mount Mabu in 2007–8. While Namuli is higher and boasts a larger massif with more diverse habitat, Mabu – less steep and with more soil on its flanks – turned out to be harbouring a 'lost' forest. With the help of satellite imagery provided by Google Earth, Bayliss identified this mountainside old-growth rainforest as one previously unknown to the scientific community. It had served as a hideout for villagers during Mozambique's civil war but had since remained uninhabited. Here the teams discovered a previously unknown species of bush viper, several new species of butterfly, and many undocumented plant varieties.

Mount Namuli can offer even more to the scientific community. 'There's a much greater diversity of habitat on Namuli,' said Timberlake. 'It is that little bit higher, and so the lie of the rock is such that you get these unique grasslands developing: trees can't grow because the soil is waterlogged, and built up into peat. So you have these peat grasslands, which are very unusual in the tropics.'

In the years since his first expedition, Namuli is facing more development pressures. 'When we were on Namuli in 2007, there were quite a few wild pigs up there grazing and they've been removed now, but people have moved in, big time, in the last ten years, to grow potatoes. To do this they clear patches of forest by cutting and burning. But the crop only lasts for a couple of years and they move on, so there's been quite a bit of forest lost in this way. The potatoes are a pretty lucrative crop – they can transport them down on a motorbike to the nearest town and get far more money than they could by working in fields with maize. So the real threat to Namuli is from semi-commercial farming.'

MOUNTAINS AS SERVICE PROVIDERS

I asked Timberlake why preserving these sorts of mountain systems should be a priority. He explained that mountains in general provide ecosystem services that might not be immediately apparent. 'As moist air comes in from the Indian Ocean, it rises over these mountains, cools and forms clouds and releases moisture. So a lot of these mountain areas produce a disproportionate amount of water in the form of rainfall in this region, which of course gets used downstream for cities and towns. And if you removed vegetation from the slopes of these mountains, you wouldn't get that same level of precipitation because the rock would be too warm and you won't get that cloud formation to anywhere near the same extent.'

Another service mountains provide is less tangible, and points again to the importance of conservation. 'I think mountains by their nature can be very inspirational – they are places of relative calm and solace,' said Timberlake. 'They provide focal points for tourism and in terms of their area, they're relatively limited. So if one conserves and looks after these patches, you're getting a bigger bang for your buck, rather than large swaths of lower elevation land. And of course because they're rugged, steep, and have high rainfall or shallow or poorer-drained soils, mountains are not in demand for agriculture in many cases. If you took away good fertile soil from people who wanted to grow maize it would be a bit of a struggle, but if you've got areas where you can't grow maize anyway, it's easier to justify value from a conservation standpoint.'

CLIMBING FOR CONSERVATION

A few years after Timberlake's expeditions to Mozambique, a young American climber named Majka Burhardt contacted him. She'd read reports on Namuli and Mabu and wanted to gather a team to climb them to study biodiversity as high up as possible. Timberlake knew Mabu wasn't climbable as it had no steep rock faces, but Namuli did. Thus Timberlake became a consultant to Burhardt's climbing-and-conservation project, which was soon dubbed Legado, after the Portuguese word for 'legacy', and they mounted an expedition to Namuli in 2014 to study mountainside habitats.

As the lead climber, Burhardt had no trifling responsibility guiding non-climbing scientists and a film crew up the largely unexplored monolith. The expedition checked off some notable discoveries: a new and as-yet-unidentified species of snake, a previously unknown caecilian (a rare snake-like amphibian), and 40 ant genera, including several unidentified species.

The expedition reinforced for biologists around the world that this lush inselberg is an untapped goldmine in the sky. The expedition's success taking non-climbing scientists safely up an unexplored rock face set a precedent in research-driven exploration.

Another part of the project reached out to the communities living around the mountain. Burhardt explained that biodiversity protection is only one aspect of the mission. 'We also need to develop a plan that advances human livelihood. It's not a pristine mountain with no human involvement – it's very much peoples' backyard...We're coming out of a time where the only option for protection was to create a national park. We need a more nimble solution. What we're hoping for is something small-scale and replicable that can then be adapted in other areas.'

SAVING 'SKY ISLANDS'

Legado's consulting scientists, including Jonathan Timberlake, have identified 48 more 'sky islands' across the region. ('Sky Islands' is also a term used specifically for the lush ranges rising over 1,800 metres (5,900 feet) above the desert of southeastern Arizona and northern Mexico, harbouring plants and animals that would not find habitat in the desert below. But for Legado's purposes, 'sky islands' is a general term to describe the inselbergs in the Eastern Afromontane.)

Burhardt explained how the concept fits into the Legado Initiative: 'a sky island is a mountain that has exceptionally large biodiversity in an exceptionally small area, like Mount Namuli. In Mozambique, these mountains account for only 0.3 per cent of the landmass yet have over 20 per cent of all of the country's bird species, and 60 per cent of its butterflies. Additionally, each of these mountains supplies water to millions of people downstream.' Burhardt and team continue to gather and analyze data on the mountains' water catchment. 'These mountains are water towers for their surroundings,' said Burhardt, 'and with a surge of interest in protecting water sources, I think it's critical to give these mountains their full hydrological credit.'

Burhardt added that there are undoubtedly temperate mountain systems around the world that have not been recognized as biodiversity hotspots. 'At present, I think there are many mountains that have not been recognized for their combined biodiversity and ecosystem-services importance. There's a great opportunity – and a need – to work in those areas today. Here is the thing about mountain conservation thus far: many places which have been conserved are not the mountains with the most biodiversity, but rather the most amazing vistas, skylines, and more. Shifting to a lower-altitude, species-rich view of mountain conservation will shift the needle on total biodiversity conservation.'

~~~~~~~~~~

Fanjingshan: Another Sky Island Recognized

Global biodiversity received another boost in 2018 when the United Nations Educational, Scientific and Cultural Organization (UNESCO) picked Fanjingshan, a series of peaks in the Wuling Mountains of southwestern China, as one of its World Heritage Sites.

UNESCO's World Heritage mandate 'seeks to encourage the identification, protection and preservation of cultural and natural heritage around the world considered to be of outstanding value to humanity.' Fanjingshan is clearly a 'sky island': the UNESCO decision describes it as 'an island of metamorphic rock in a sea of karst, home to many plant and animal species that originated in the Tertiary period, between 65 million and 2 million years ago.' Though this sounds a bit like *The Lost World* – Arthur Conan Doyle's 1912 novel about a valley where dinosaurs still roam, and an inspiration to the *Jurassic Park* films – Fanjingshan is not pristinely wild. Several Ming Dynasty-era Buddhist temples and associated buildings can be found there. 'Fanjingshan' refers to the massif and locale but there are three main pillar-like summits, each one topped with a temple; the Golden Summit is the highest, at 2,572 metres (8,400 feet) above sea level.

Isolation has preserved much ultra-rare biodiversity here, including the subtropical conifer forests with the endemic Fanjingshan Fir (*Abies fanjingshanensis*) and Guizhou Snub-nosed Monkey (*Rhinopithecus brelichi*), and the endangered Forest Musk Deer (*Moschus berezovskii*) and Chinese Giant Salamander (*Andrias davidianus*). Fanjingshan also boasts an old-growth beech forest. Researchers have recorded 3,724 plant species here so far, an incredible 13 per cent of China's flora just in this relatively small area.[56] Hopefully this and other high-altitude conservation efforts will lead humanity to the realization that mountains aren't just for climbing.

~~~~~~~~~~

What Can We Do for Mountains?

Mountains can help us to learn about ourselves and our place in the continuum of earth's biosphere. In all their geographical and ecological variety, mountains hold sway over our climate, water resources and the integrity of earth's biodiversity. They also influence our health and wellbeing in ways we're just beginning to understand. One of the athletes interviewed for this book, ski-mountaineer Greg Hill (*see* page 87), spoke about his on-slope adventures as a process of peeling back layers to reveal his core self, finally unencumbered and free. Perhaps mountains can do all of us a comparable service.

So what can we do for mountains? We can support public parks and national parks in mountain regions by visiting them, and leave no trace during our stay. We can also donate to or volunteer for environmental, land stewardship or conservation organizations. With world population projected to reach almost 10 billion by 2050, mountain regions – due to their relative inaccessibility – may be some of the last places to face extreme settlement and development pressures. That's why it should be our present task to conserve them in perpetuity.

Though earth's high ranges may seem impossibly remote – the wind-scoured snowfields and crags splendid in their barren isolation – in fact we're all connected to them in a myriad of ways.

Mountains are landforms and ecosystems as complex and distinctive as the humans who live among them or in their shadow. Raising public awareness about the vulnerability of our remaining hinterlands is one way to give back to the places that give us so much and joining your local trekking or hillwalking club will give you more than just peace of mind and physical fitness.

Wilderness is worth saving on its own merits, and also for a more selfish reason: because it will save us in return.

REFERENCES

1 Director L Guthman (2002) *Messner.* https://youtu.be/YVYDVUbHIK4

2 Anker, C et al (2013) *The Call of Everest: The History, Science, and Future of the World's Tallest Peak*

3 https://www.mountaineers.org/blog/to-everest-and-beyond-tom-hornbein-reflects-on-life-and-mountains

4 https://www.nytimes.com/1998/03/14/world/lerik-journal-yogurt-caucasus-centenarians-never-eat-it.html **and** https://www.nytimes.com/1971/12/26/archives/why-they-live-to-be-100-or-even-older-in-abkhasia-faces-in-an.html

5 Baibas, N, Trichopoulou, A et al (2005) Residence in mountainous compared with lowland areas in relation to total and coronary mortality. A study in rural Greece. *Journal of Epidemiology and Community Health* 59(4) 274–278

6 https://www.mayoclinic.org/diseases-conditions/metabolic-syndrome/symptoms-causes/syc-20351916

7 Lopez-Pascual, A et al (2016) Living at a geographically higher elevation is associated with lower risk of metabolic syndrome: prospective analysis of the SUN cohort. *Frontiers in Physiology* 7:658

8 Palmer, B and Clegg, D (2014) Ascent to altitude as a weight loss method: The good and bad of hypoxia inducible factor activation. *Obesity (Silver Spring)* 22(2): 311–317

9 Voss, J, Allison, D et al (2014) Lower obesity rate during residence at high altitude among a military population with frequent migration: A quasi experimental model for investigating spatial causation. *PLoS One* 9(4):e93493

10 Faeh, D, Moser, A, Panczak R et al (2016) Independent at heart: Persistent association of altitude with ischaemic heart disease mortality

after consideration of climate, topography and built environment. *J Epidemiol Community Health* 70: 798–806

11 Woolcott, O et al (2015) Glucose homeostasis during short-term and prolonged exposure to high altitudes. *Endocr Rev* 36(2): 149–173

12 Burtscher, M (2014) Effects of living at higher altitudes on mortality: A narrative review. *Aging Dis* 5(4): 274–280

13 Park, BJ, Miyazaki, Y et al (2007) Physiological effects of shinrin-yoku (taking in the atmosphere of the forest) using salivary cortisol and cerebral activity as indicators. *Journal of Physiological Anthropology* 26(2): 123–128

14 Kuo, M (2015) How might contact with nature promote human health? Promising mechanisms and a possible central pathway. *Frontiers in Psychology* 6:1093

15 Joye, Y and Bolderdijk, JW (2014) An exploratory study into the effects of extraordinary nature on emotions, mood, and prosociality. *Frontiers in Psychology* 5: 1577

16 https://www.sciencealert.com/doctors-in-scotland-are-literally-prescribing-nature-to-patients-shetland-gps-pilot-benefits-health-mental

17 Williams, PT and Thompson, PD (2013) Walking versus running for hypertension, cholesterol, and diabetes mellitus risk reduction. *Arterioscler Thromb Vasc Biol* 33(5): 1085–1091

18 Focht, BC (2009) Brief walks in outdoor and laboratory environments: Effects on affective responses, enjoyment, and intentions to walk for exercise. *Research Quarterly for Exercise and Sport* 80: 611–620

19 https://cvmbs.source.colostate.edu/a-17000-foot-view-csu-researcher-finds-surprising-results-in-high-altitude-study/

20 Chicco, A et al (2018) Adaptive remodeling of skeletal muscle energy metabolism in high-altitude hypoxia: Lessons from AltitudeOmics. *J Biol Chem* 293(1): 6659–6671

21 Husaini, A (Ed) *Medicinal Plants of the Himalayas: Advances and Insights.* Global Science Books 2010

22 Rudd, M et al (2018) Inspired to create: Awe enhances openness to learning and the desire for experiential creation. *Journal of Marketing Research* 55(3): 002224371880285

23 Atchley, RA, Strayer, DL and Atchley, P (2012) Creativity in the wild: Improving creative reasoning through immersion in natural settings. *PLoS One* 7(12): e51474

24 Jakubec, S (2016) Mental well-being and quality-of-life benefits of inclusion in nature for adults with disabilities and their caregivers. *Landscape Research* 41(6): 616–627 and http://canadianmountainnetwork.ca/2016/09/30/mountains-nature-experiences-improve-mental-well-being/

25 Selhub, E and Logan, A *Your Brain on Nature: the Science of Nature's Influence on Your Health, Happiness and Vitality.* Collins, 2014

26 Aspinall, P and Mavros, P (2015) The urban brain: Analysing outdoor physical activity with mobile EEG. *Br J Sports Med* 49(4): 272–276

27 Blumenthal, J, Babyak, M, Doraiswamy, PM et al (2007) Exercise and pharmacotherapy in the treatment of major depressive disorder. *Psychosom Med* 69(7): 587–596

28 Ratey, J, *Spark: The Revolutionary New Science of Exercise and the Brain.* Little, Brown and Company, 2008

29 http://www.pbs.org/wnet/americanmasters/john-muir-in-the-new-world-read-a-biographical-essay-john-muir-natures-witness/1806/

30 https://www.nps.gov/thri/johnmuir.htm

31 Muir, John, *My First Summer in the Sierra (With Original Drawings & Photographs), Adventure Memoirs, Travel Sketches & Wilderness Studies*

32 https://www.fs.usda.gov/recarea/inyo/recarea/?recid=21875

33 https://www.wilderness.net/nwps/legisact?print=yes

34 http://www.grossnationalhappiness.com/wp-content/uploads/2017/01/Final-GNH-Report-jp-21.3.17-ilovepdf-compressed.pdf

35 https://www.mountaineers.org/blog/to-everest-and-beyond-tom-hornbein-reflects-on-life-and-mountains

36 https://research.noaa.gov/article/ArtMID/587/ArticleID/2362/Another-climate-milestone-falls-at-NOAA%E2%80%99s-Mauna-Loa-observatory

37 https://phys.org/news/2013-05-one-third-sea-mountain-glaciers.html#jCp

38 Carlson, L, Speca, M, Faris, P and Patel, K (2007) One year pre–post intervention follow-up of psychological, immune, endocrine and blood pressure outcomes of mindfulness-based stress reduction (MBSR) in breast and prostate cancer outpatients. *Brain Behaviour Immunity* 21: 1038–1049

39 Hofmann, S, Sawyer, A, Witt, A and Oh, D (2010) The effect of mindfulness-based therapy on anxiety and depression: A meta-analytic review. *Journal of Consulting and Clinical Psychology* 78: 169–183

40 Brewer, J, Sinha, R, Chen, J et al (2009) Mindfulness training and stress reactivity in substance abuse: Results from a randomized, controlled stage I pilot study. *Substance Abuse* 30: 306–317

41 Campbell, T, Labelle, L, Bacon, S,

Faris, P and Carlson, L (2012) Impact of mindfulness-based stress reduction (MBSR) on attention, rumination and resting blood pressure in women with cancer: A waitlist-controlled study. *Journal of Behavioural Medicine* 35: 262–271

42 Fredrickson, B, Cohn, M, Coffey, K, Pek, J and Finkel, S (2008) Open hearts build lives: Positive emotions, induced through loving-kindness meditation, build consequential personal resources. *Journal of Personality and Social Psychology* 95: 1045–1062

43 Bostanov, V, Keune, P, Kotchoubey, B and Hautzinger, M (2012) Event-related brain potentials reflect increased concentration ability after mindfulness-based cognitive therapy for depression: A randomized clinical trial. *Psychiatry Research* 199(3): 174–180 and Mrazek, M, Franklin, M, Phillips, D, Baird, B and Schooler, J (2013) Mindfulness training improves working memory capacity and performance while reducing mind wandering. *Psychological Science* 24: 776–781

44 Holzel, B et al (2011) Mindfulness practice leads to increases in regional brain grey matter density. *Psychiatry Resources* 191: 36–43

45 Orme-Johnson, DW. (1987) Medical care utilisation and the transcendental meditation programme. *Psychocomatic Medicine* 49: 493–507 and Goyal, M, Singh, S, Sibinga, EM et al (2014) Meditation programs for psychological stress and well-being: A systematic review and meta-analysis. *JAMA Internal Medicine* 174(3): 357–68

46 Keltner, D (2016) Why do we feel awe? Retrieved from http://www.mindful.org/why-do-we-feel-awe/

47 Van den Berg, M, Maas, J et al (2015) Autonomic nervous system responses to viewing green and built settings: Differentiating

between sympathetic and parasympathetic activity *Int J Environ Res Public Health* 12(12): 15860–15874

48 Tadić, V, Jeremic, I et al (2012) Anti-inflammatory, gastroprotective, and cytotoxic effects of Sideritis scardica extracts. *Planta Medica* 78(5): 415–427

49 Hofrichter, J, Krohn, M et al (2016) Sideritis spp. extracts enhance memory and learning in Alzheimer's ß-amyloidosis mouse models and aged C57Bl/6 mice. *J Alzheimers Dis* 53(3): 967–980

50 Igarashi, M, Miyazaki, Y et al (2014) Effects of olfactory stimulation with rose and orange oil on prefrontal cortex activity. *Complement Ther Med* 22(6) 1027–1031 and Miyazaki, Y et al (1992) Changes in mood by inhalation of essential oils by humans II. Effects of essential oils on blood pressure, heart rate, R–R intervals, performance, sensory evaluation and POMS. *Mokuzai Gakkaishi* 38: 909–913 (in Japanese with English abstract)

51 http://www.bbc.com/future/story/20170227-how-tibetans-survive-life-on-the-roof-of-the-world

52 http://www.actionbioscience.org/evolution/beall.html

53 Willie, CK et al (2016) UBC-Nepal expedition: An experimental overview of the 2016 University of British Columbia scientific expedition to Nepal Himalaya. *PLoS One* 13(10): e0204660

54 B.C.'s Wild Harts: Yellowstone to Yukon Conservation Initiative. Retrieved from https://issuu.com/y2yinitiative/docs/y2y_wildhartsbrochure_web

55 https://gypaetebarbu.fr/life-gypconnect-en/

56 https://whc.unesco.org/en/list/1559

INDEX

A

Abkhazia 24
acclimatization to high altitude 36–7
Achenbach, Ken 102–3
Acute Mountain Sickness (AMS) 137–8
Adams, Ansel 43
adventure guiding 58–9
Alps 9, 12, 79, 168
AltitudeOmics Project 35–6
AMS (Acute Mountain Sickness) 137–8
Andean mint 150
Andes 12, 72
 Bolivian 35–6, 38–9
 Chimborazo 72–4
animals
 Eastern Afromontane 174
 Fanjingshan 181
 Legado expedition 179
 Y2Y initiative 160, 162, 164–5, 166, 170, 172
 lammergeyers 168–9
anti-ageing products 147
anxiety reduction 115, 117, 123
art and the sublime 44–5
Australia 167
awe 45–6, 49–51
 awe-inspiring activities 130

B

B2B (Baja to Bering Marine Priority Conservation Area) 167
Bayliss, Dr Julian 176
Beall, Cynthia 156
bearded vultures 168–9
bears 160, 164–5, 166
Begbie, Mount 90
Bhutan 84
biodiversity 12, 173–81, 182
 Eastern Afromontane 173–80
 Himalayas 40
 Legado expedition 179
 Sierra Nevada 75
 sky islands 179–81
 Y2Y initiative 166–7, 172
Blackcomb (Hortsman) Glacier 98, 102–3
Blake, William 11
Bolivian Andes 35–6, 38–9

Brain-Derived Neurotrophic Factor (BDNF) 69
brain fatigue 67
breathing 129, 136
British Columbia 55
 Blackcomb Mountain 98, 102–3
 Darkwoods Conservation Area 172
 Monashee Range 88
 Peace River Break 161–2
 Selkirk Mountains 9
 Whistler 62, 63, 65, 129
Buddhism 84, 122, 181
 sacred mountains 16, 19, 53
 Tibetan 19, 24, 83, 122
Burhardt, Majka 178–80
Burke, Edmund 44
Burkhart, Tim 161

C

Cabinet-Purcell Mountain Corridor 164
Caldwell, Tommy 82
Camp of Champions 102–3
Canigou, Mount 16–17
caribou 170, 172
Cartaya, Eddy 105
Cascade Mountains 105, 153
Catalans 16–17
Caucasus Mountains 24, 25
caving 105–9
cedars 149
CEPF (Critical Ecosystem Partnership Fund) 173, 174
Chacaltaya, Mount 36
Chicco, Adam 36–7, 39
Child, Greg 141
Chimborazo 72–4
Chinese medicine (TCM) 64–5
Chouinard, Yvon 83, 91
climate change 79, 90, 98, 99, 100–3
 carbon dioxide emissions 100–2
 in glacier caves 105, 108
 melting glaciers 102–3
 Y2Y initiative and resilience to 165, 166–7
climbers 14, 19
 free-soloing 82–3
 and self-examination 20–1
 waterfall climbing 109
climbing 34, 68, 133, 135
climbing walls 143
conservation 72, 133, 173, 178
 Eastern Afromontane 174–5

Legado expedition 178–80
 in Ode to Muir 79–80
 see also biodiversity; Y2Y (Yellowstone to Yukon)
Corbett, Barry 20–1
cortisol 114
creativity 45–51, 123
 creative pursuits 112–13
The Cross in the Mountains (Friedrich) 44

D

Dalai Lama 122
Darkwoods Conservation Area 172
deaths
 climbers 19, 20
 hypoxia-related 156
 mortality and high altitudes 24, 30
Denmark 56
depression 32, 68, 87, 115
development pressures 170
diabetes 26, 30, 34
disabilities, adults with 61
discomfort of mountains 55, 58–9

E

Eastern Afromontane 173–80
ecosystem services 12–13
edelweiss 147
8, 000ers 19, 20
environmental footprints 98–9
essential oils 148–51
Ethiopian wolf 174
Everest 54, 84, 142
 climbing 19, 20–1
exercise 24, 27, 29
 energetic activities 132–6
 for health and wellbeing 34–5, 67–9
 mountain fitness at home 143
 in nature 35, 143
extreme sports 80

F

The Fall of an Avalanche in the Grisons (Turner) 45
Fanjingshan 181
flow state 94–7
forest bathing 31
forest fires 98
Friedrich, Caspar David 44
Fuji, Mount 52–4

G

Gangkhar Puensum, Bhutan 84
genetics, high-altitude 156–9
glaciers 13, 58, 80, 90
  exploring caves 105–9
  melting 102–3
González-Muniesa, Pedro 26
The Great Wave Off Kanagawa
  (Hokusai) 53
Greece 24
Greek myth 14
grizzly bears 164–5, 166
Gross National Happiness
  Index 84

H

haikus 113
happiness 123
health and wellbeing 23–41, 182
  and biodiversity loss 173
  hypoxia 35–7, 156, 158
  longevity 24
  mountain exercise 34–5
  mountain tea 146
  plants 40–1, 147
  weight loss 26, 29
  see also mental wellbeing
heart disease 26, 30, 32, 34
  and hypoxia 37, 156
Heisig, James 54
Herbert, T.M. 83
highest mountains 12, 74
hiking 34, 69, 132, 133, 134
Hillary, Edmund 19, 20
Hill, Greg 87–90, 182
Hilty, Dr Jodi 161, 162, 164–5, 166–7,
  170, 172
Himalayan cedar 149
Himalayas 12, 13, 14, 54
  Bhutan 84–5
  climbers 19
  medicinal plants 40–1
  and meditation 122
  Shambhala 83
Hindus 13, 14
Hokusai, Katsushika 53
Holocene period 102
Honnold, Alex 82
Hornbein, Thomas 20–1
Hortsman (Blackcomb) Glacier 98,
  102–3
human interaction 97
Humboldt, Alexander von 72–4
Hydeman, Josh 105–9

hydroelectricity 13
hypoxia 35–7, 156, 158

I

Ibsen, Henrik 56
Illecillewaet Glacier 58, 90
images of mountains 142
immune system 32, 115, 123
indigenous populations 13, 170
  genetic research on 156–9
industrial development 161, 170
inselbergs 179
ironwort 146

J

Jabal al-Nūr 14
Japan 31, 52–4
Jason, in Greek myth 14
Jones, Jeremy 79, 80
Jorgeson, Kevin 82
Journal of Marketing Research 47
Jurassic Park films 181

K

K2 19
Kailash, Mount 18–19
Keeling, Charles David 100, 102
Keeling, Ralph 102
Kew, Royal Botanical Gardens 175
Kirkby, Bruce 55, 58–60
Korea 16
Kyrgyzstan 17

L

lakes 130
lammergeyers 168–9
landscape painters 144–5
Last Frontier Heliskiing 137
lavender essential oil 149–50
Le, Catherine 36
Legado expedition 178–80
Lincoln, Abraham 77
The Living Mountain (Shepherd) 7
Logan, Mount 137
longevity 24
Lopez-Pascual, Amaya 27
Lost Horizon (Hilton) 83
The Lost World (Conan Doyle) 181

M

Mabu, Mount 176, 178
McGregor, Brent 105
Mahabharata 13
Mauna Loa, Hawaii 100–2
medicinal plants 40–1
meditation 114, 122–5

mental wellbeing 32, 43–69
  activities 114–29
  awe and the sublime 44–6
  creativity 45–6, 47–51
  discomfort 55, 58–9
  and mountain exercise 67–9
  the 'reinvented self' 61
  respect for mountains 62–5
Messner, Reinhold 20, 79
metabolic syndrome 26–7
MFR (Marie-France Roy) 91–9
mindfulness 114–21
  benefits of 115
  exercises 120–1
  research 117
monasteries 16
montane forests 173
Mont Blanc 19, 88, 138, 139
Morning in the Riesengebirge
  (Friedrich) 44
Moses 14
mountain gorilla 174
mountain pose (Tadasana) 126–7
Mozambique 174–5, 176, 180
mugwort 41
Muhammad, Prophet 14
Muir, John 23, 72–83, 112, 155
  free-solo climbing 82–3
  on the incense cedar 153
  John Muir Wilderness 79–80
  The Mountains of California 80–2
  My First Summer in the Sierra 77, 78,
    82
  Ode to Muir film 79–82
  Our National Parks 153
  The Yosemite 82
Muses 13
Myers, Norman 173
myths 13–14, 24

N

Namuli, Mount 174–5, 176, 177, 180
Norgay, Sherpa Tenzing 19
Norway 56

O

Olympic National Park (USA) 92–5
Olympus 13

P

painting 112
  landscape painters 144–5
Papoose Cave 108–9
Paquet, Dr Paul 160
Patagonia (manufacturer) 83, 91, 92

Pelion, Mount 14
pennell 40
Peruvian pink pepper 150–1
Pflitsch, Andreas 105, 108
photography 106–8, 113
pilgrimages 14, 16–17, 19
Fuji 53, 54
plants
Eastern Afromontane 174
edelweiss 147
Fanjingshan 181
medicinal 40–1
mountain tea 146
poetry 113
population growth 182
POW (Protect Our Winters) 79, 90,
99
problem solving 51, 68, 113
Proctor, Dr Michael 164
Protect Our Winters (POW) 79, 90,
99
Pyrénées 169

Q
Qibo, Chinese physician 65

R
rainfall 178
Rainier, Mount 45–6, 50, 108
research, genetic 156–9
respect for mountains 62–5
Revelstoke 90
rivers 13
Rocky Mountains 12, 61, 79, 90
Y2Y initiative 160, 161
Romanticism 44
Roosevelt, Theodore 77–8
Rowell, Galen 79
Rudd, Melanie 45–6, 47–51
Ruskin, John 71

S
sacred mountains 13, 16–19
Mount Fuji 52–4
Sandy Glacier caves 105, 106
Sansa Monasteries 16
Scandinavians and friluftsliv 56
Scotland 32
self-awareness 68
self-esteem 67, 68, 115, 123
self-examination 20–1
self-heal plant 40–1
self-knowledge 86–9
self-reliance 88–9

sequioia trees 75, 77
services provided by
mountains 178
Seven Dials Mountains 108
Shambhala 24, 83
Shangri-La 83
Sherpas 158, 159
Shinto 53, 54
Sierra Nevada 74–9, 80, 82, 153
Sinai 14
sketching 112
skiing 34, 68, 132, 134, 137–8
dry slopes 143
ski-mountaineering 86–9
sky islands 179–81
sleep 27, 31, 32, 34, 65
snowboarding 62–4, 80, 91
dry slopes 143
health benefits of 34, 68, 134
MFR on 91–5
snowpack 13
solitude 39
star-gazing 130
stress 32, 68, 129
reduction 114, 115, 117, 123, 142
the sublime 44–6
Sulaiman-Too Mountain 17
sustainable development 84
Sweden 56

T
Ta'c Wees cave 108–9
Tans, Pieter 100
tea 146
technology 51, 112
Tenzing Norgay 19, 20
The Tetschen Altar (Friedrich) 44
Thirty-Six Views of Mount Fuji
(Hokusai) 53
Thoreau, Henry David 78
Tibetans
Buddhists 19, 24, 83, 122
high-altitude genetics 156
Timberlake, Jonathan 175–6, 178
time-perception and awe 46, 50
tourism 13, 178
travelling to high altitude 137–8
trees 153
Turner, Joseph 46
Tymko, Michael 158–9

U
Umpleby, Cliff 137, 138
uncertainty, savouring 20–1

UNESCO World Heritage Sites 16,
181
United States
National Parks movement 72, 78,
79–80, 160
Wilderness Act (1964) 80
see also Y2Y (Yellowstone to Yukon)
Unsoeld, Willi 20, 21
urban living 58–9, 60

V
Vallée, Dominique 62–5, 129
Vaux, Mary 90
virtual reality (VR) 142
visualization 144

W
walking 34, 35, 67, 68, 134
water 12–13, 130, 167, 178, 182
sky islands 180
waterfalls 109, 130
weight loss and altitude 26, 29
wellbeing activities, *see also* mental
wellbeing
Whistler, British Columbia 62, 63
Whitney, Mount 75, 83
wilderness snowboarding 92–5
writing 113
Wurst, Jeff 109
Württemberg, Duke Carl Herzog
von 172

X
X Games 91

Y
Y2Y (Yellowstone to Yukon) 160–73
biodiversity 166–7, 172
and climate change 166–7
connecting landscapes 161–2,
167–9
Darkwoods Conservation
Area 172
Peace River Break 161–2
wildlife conservation 160, 162,
164–5, 166
Yellowstone National Park 80
yoga 114, 126–9
Yosemite National Park 75–7, 78,
82–3, 153

Z
Zahniser, Howard 80

FURTHER READING

BOOKS

– Anker, C et al *The Call of Everest: The History, Science, and Future of the World's Tallest Peak*. National Geographic Books, 2013

– Armstrong, Karen *A Short History of Myth*. Canongate, 2006

– Bernbaum, Edwin *The Way to Shambhala: A Search for the Mythical Kingdom Beyond the Himalayas*. Shambhala, 2001

– Besel, RD and Bernard K Duffy (Eds) *Green Voices: Defending Nature and the Environment in American Civic Discourse*. SUNY Press, 2016

– Burke, Edmund *A Philosophical Enquiry into the Origins of the Sublime and Beautiful and Other Pre-Revolutionary Writings*. Penguin Classics, 1999

– Eliade, Mircea *Patterns in Comparative Religion*. Bison Books, 1996

– Hornbein, Thomas *Everest: the West Ridge*. Mountaineers Books, 2013

– Husaini, Amjad (Ed) *Medicinal Plants of the Himalayas: Advances and Insights*. Global Science Books, 2010

– Jones, Marjorie *The Life and Times of Mary Vaux Walcott*. Schiffer, 2015

– Kaiser, James *Yosemite: The Complete Guide*. Destination Press, 2011

– Keyes, Roger *Hokusai: Beyond the Great Wave*. Thames and Hudson, 2017

– Macfarlane, Robert *Mountains of the Mind*. Vintage, 2004

– Messner, Reinhold and Thomas Huetlin *Reinhold Messner: My Life at the Limit*. Mountaineers Books, 2014

– Muir, John *Journeys in the Wilderness: A John Muir Reader*. Birlinn Ltd, 2009

– Price, Martin (Ed) *Mountain Geography: Physical and Human Dimensions*. University of California Press, 2013

– Ratey, John *Spark: The Revolutionary New Science of Exercise and the Brain*. Quercus, 2013

– Selhub, E and Logan, A *Your Brain on Nature: The Science of Nature's Influence on Your Health, Happiness and Vitality*. Collins, 2014

– Thoreau, Henry David *The Portable Thoreau*. Penguin Classics, 2012

– Verschuuren, Bas and Naoya Furuta (Eds) *Asian Sacred Natural Sites: Philosophy and Practice in Protected Areas and Conservation*. Routledge, 2016

– Wolfe, Linnie Marsh *Son of the Wilderness: The Life of John Muir*. University of Wisconsin Press, 1945, 1973

– Wulf, Andrea *The Invention of Nature: Alexander Von Humboldt's New World*. Vintage, 2016

WEBSITES

– Bhutan and Gross National Happiness: www.grossnationalhappiness.com

– Climber Majka Burhardt: www.majkaburhardt.com

– Conservation International: www.conservation.org

– Critical Ecosystem Partnership Fund: www.cepf.net

– Ski mountaineer Greg Hill: www.greghill.ca

– Josh Hydeman Photography: www.joshhydeman.com

– IUCN Redlist of Threatened Species: www.iucnredlist.org

– Royal Botanic Gardens, Kew: www.kew.org

– Adventurer Bruce Kirkby: www.brucekirkby.com

– Landscape and the Sublime: www.bl.uk/romantics-and-victorians/articles/landscape-and-the-sublime

– Last Frontier Heliskiing: www.lastfrontierheli.com

– Legado Mozambican conservation project: www.legadoinitiative.org

– Mauna Loa Observatory atmospheric research facility: www.esrl.noaa.gov/gmd/obop/mlo

– Mountain stats and climbing info: www.summitpost.org / www.mountaineers.org

– Oregon State University Volcano World: http://volcano.oregonstate.edu

– Patagonia, the environmental activist company: www.patagonia.com/the-activist-company.html

– Protect Our Winters charity: www.protectourwinters.uk / www.protectourwinters.org / www.protectourwinters.ca

– The Sierra Club John Muir exhibit: http://vault.sierraclub.org/john_muir_exhibit

– Teton Gravity Research films: www.tetongravity.com

– UNESCO World Heritage Site Guide: https://whc.unesco.org

– US National Parks Service resources on Yosemite and John Muir: www.nps.gov/yose/learn/historyculture/muir.htm

– World Heath Organization resources on biodiversity: www.who.int/globalchange/ecosystems/biodiversity

– World Wildlife Fund: www.worldwildlife.org

– Yellowstone to Yukon Conservation Initiative: www.y2y.net

PICTURE CREDITS

Alamy Stock Photo Hugh Pearson/Nature Picture Library 177.

iStock AndrewSoundarajan 74; Bartosz Hadyniak 157; borchee 186; cheechew 85; ChrisPelle 139; Creativaimage 96; Daniel_Kay 33; deimagine 9; DenisTangneyJr 128; DieterMeyrl 125; ePhotocorp 149; FabioFilzi 131; Jason_V 164; juliannafunk 126; kokoroyuki 52; Lukas Bischoff 183; Mantonature 41; Marina_Poushkina 30; Martinelli73 38; maurusasdf 174; MikeLane45 168; Mumemories 36; myshkovsky 25; mzabarovsky 21; Pgiam 152; primeimages 45; R.M. Nunes 158; RPBMedia 150; Samson1976 93; Sebastian_man 18; stockstudioX 63, 114; tanukiphoto 147; VisualCommunications 116; wwing 171; ZargonDesign 86.

Josh Hydeman 104, 107.

Unsplash Ales Krivec 120; Antonio Molinari 66; Ashim D'Silva 28; Chris Lawton 81; Drew Collins 48; Hendrik Morkel 57; Johannes Andersson 163; Josh Carter 76; Kalen Emsley 58; Luca Zanon 64; Marc Steenbeke 15; Oldskool Photography 2; Paul Summers 73; Stephan Seeber 88; Steve Halama 101; Thomas Griesbeck 145.

ACKNOWLEDGEMENTS

The author wishes to thank the following people who directly or indirectly helped bring this book into the light:

Kate Adams, Leslie Anthony, Tom Appleyard, Charles Austin, Dave Baines, Feet Banks, Steven Bray, Jon Burak, Majka Burhardt, Margaret and Scott Cameron, Melanie Chambers, Adam Chicco, Wendy Clark, Kelly Culbertson, David Erb, Flavia Esteves, Colin Field, Joel Forrest, Bruce Geddes, Daryl Greaser, Jim Greenlaw, Bryan Grundmann, Charlie and Ella Garrad, Glen Harris, Kim Harris, Greg Hill, Jeff Howard, Amelie Legare, Jodi Hilty, Josh Hydeman, Grant Kearns, Bruce Kirkby, Rheanna Kish, Michael Koehle, Todd Lawson, Catherine Le, Dave Loopstra, Pedro González Muniesa, Scott MacGregor, Drew McIvor, Louise McKeever, Cameron McKittrick, Katherine McKittrick, Carol and Chris Mills, Ella Morgan, Jack and Linda Morgan, Joan Morgan, Jonny Morgan, Josh Morgan, Sarah Morgan, John Moss, Nick Pairaudeau, Caroline Paquin, Kevin Paquin, Nate Paquin, Scott Parent, Al Phillips, Stuart Phillips, Robert Plowman, Audrey Potter, Bruce Potter, Jane Potter, Marilyn Potter, Susan Potter, Esther Regenwetter, Robert Roach, Alison Ronson, Skip Ross, Steve Rosset, Marie-France Roy, Dan Rubinstein, Melanie Rudd, Marsha Russell, Randy Schwartz, Diane Shaw, Bill Steele, Jack Storey, Mike Strimas, Rick Taylor, Jonathan Timberlake, Mike Tymko, Cliff Umpleby, Dominique Vallee, Ed Viesturs, George Weider, Mark Zelinski, Kelly Zenkewich.

The author would also like to thank Jo Smith for her contributions on pages 24 (bottom), 31, 34, 35 (top), 40 (top), 44 (top), 51 (bottom), 56, 67–8, 97 (top), 112–27, 130–6, 142–51 and 169.